Just When I Thought My Life Was Over God Spoke And Said Where Art Thou?

GOD HEARS MY VOICE

CHADEOSIYIA J BROWN

Chadeosiyia B. Publishing Company

Just When I Thought My Life Was Over God Spoke And Said Where Art Thou?
God Hears My Voice
All Rights Reserved.
Copyright © 2026 Chadeosiyia J Brown
v5.0

The opinions expressed in this manuscript are solely the opinions of the author and do not represent the opinions or thoughts of the publisher. The author has represented and warranted full ownership and/or legal right to publish all the materials in this book.

This book may not be reproduced, transmitted, or stored in whole or in part by any means, including graphic, electronic, or mechanical without the express written consent of the publisher except in the case of brief quotations embodied in critical articles and reviews.

Chadeosiyia B. Publishing Company

ISBN: 979-8-218-80286-8

Cover Photo © 2026 www.gettyImages.com. All rights reserved - used with permission.

PRINTED IN THE UNITED STATES OF AMERICA

Acknowledgments

FIRST, I WOULD like to thank Jesus Christ in heaven my Lord and Savior for leading me, keeping me and protecting me and my family throughout our lives. Thank you Father in heaven for creating me to be the woman in Christ that I am today and for choosing me as an Ordained Minister, who serves within the communities in the highways and bi-ways where the children of God are in need. Furthermore, through many trials and struggles throughout my life, I am honored to be a born again servant, disciple and follower of Jesus Christ in heaven. My mission as a servant of Christ is to love and serve all ethnicities, races, cultures, gender and ages of God's children and to help lead as many souls to Christ, at one's willingness to serve Christ. Thank you father in heaven for creating me to be, somewhat of the Proverbs 31 woman that I am today and thank you father in heaven, for gifting me with your love, compassion and kindness to love all. Thank you father in heaven for being head of my life and my environment. Forever will I serve you and your will Lord. Amen! My acknowledgements to those who have weathered my trials with me, I dedicate this book which is a road map of my life trials and triumphs of overcoming. Firstmost, to my amazing three children: To my oldest son Deondray, (Aka "Koby") my surviving child, so wise and full of God's knowledge from deep within. Thank you, my son, for allowing me to be your mother and for teaching me how to be a first time mother during my high school years. Those were some rough years, myself being so young and not having any parenting skills, but your beautiful, little brown eyes when I looked into them when you were a baby showed me what true, unconditional love was. You nurtured me as your mother and gave me the hope and the will to continue to push forward, despite my circumstances and troubles that I faced ahead. Thank you for always telling me son as you became an adult, a husband and father with your own family, how proud you are of me and for loving me with all your heart. You have become an amazing first born son and amazing husband to my daughter in law Asia. You both are the most amazing, dedicated and committed parents to your seven children and your marriage before God. I am so proud of you son for being a better father and husband than I have ever seen with your wife and my grandchildren. Always know that no matter what, I am so proud of you, Asia and my beautiful grandchildren and I will love you all unconditionally forever and more. To my only daughter, my second born, my breath and heartbeat: My daughter Chanyka, ("Snooky "aka" CeCe") Having a daughter so precious as you are to me has made me fight, to invest my strengths as a woman with value and morals within you. You have been an example of your mother with the drive to never give up and to fight for the best for you and your only child, your son. You are an amazing mother to your son "Ronald" My handsome grandson and you both bring so much joy into my life and more. Thank you for loving me and all of my flaws unconditionally. You know that I am so proud to call you my daughter, your gifts are full and you exhibit elegance and sophistication as a "Island Queen". I am proud of you and all of your accomplishments that you have made in your life. You are a prize and God's gift, don't you ever forget your value and self-worth!. I love you daughter, forever and more. To my amazing last born child, my son Siyia: Siyia, (Aka "Buddha" aka "KS") the name your father Gerrold Mcdonald gave you that was fit for a "Black King- Siyia". Your birth put the icing on the cake, your beautiful smile and fighting spirit that you have to live is priceless! And grand!. Through all that you have had to suffer and overcome being nearly killed three times, with God protecting you each time gave me hope and stronger faith in the Lord. Your strengths and will to fight, gave me even more reasons to continue to trust God's will for our lives. You are my standby, sidekick! And I thank you for giving me the support and love that I need everyday. I am proud to have you as my son and I thank God for your life and the plans that God has for you. Your smile is captivating and puts that look of love on my face every time that I look at you, I see God's love in you. God fights for you and your siblings, so don't ever give up my baby boy. Your mother has all three of your backs, front and both sides head to toe!. I love you son forever and more: To my mother: Betty Lyn Brown, everything that I am is because of watching you and how you suffered throughout your life, but you still stood the test of time. Mama with your heart, so full of pure love and loyalty for your five children and everyone who loves you, you have always given more than you have received. Your little five feet five, one hundred and thirty five pounds plus frame, has the power when you raise your voice to scare even a bull! To silence!. Because of you mother dear, I am who I am, from watching you hold on to your faith in God. You stand as an obedient, virtuous Proverbs 31 wife and mother to us five children and our father, may he continue to rest in peace with the Lord. Life would not be life without you mama and I thank you for taking care of us five children and your grandchildren without hesitation. You have shown us all so much love and patience and you overcame so much adversity mama and daddy too. God has covered and protected you all this time coming from the segregation and Jim Crow days of Philadelphia Mississippi with our father. Thank you mama for loving me, us, like no other person on this earth has ever done before mama. I am proud to be your daughter for life! And I love you mama forever! And more!. To my father: My daddy, my ("Dee, Dee") My father, even though you have passed on to glory in rest with our savior Jesus Christ now, there is not a day that does not go by, where I don't miss you. We all wish that you were still here with me, your wife, children and grandchildren. Your strong, demanding voice, broad shoulders and muscle built frame, put many people to shame and fear at times, when you entered the room. You stood your ground and when you spoke, that is what you meant and that was the end of the story. You came from a hard past life just as mama did, raised in the segregation and Jim Crow days of Philadelphia Mississippi. The stories you both told me brought pain and shock to my soul. But, through God's grace and mercy in our lives Christ brought you and mama through the worst of it all. Thank you for loving all of me daddy, for being my father and my best friend in life, I had so much fun cooking, barbecuing and listening to the blues with you and my children. Seeing you dance with your cigar on the side of your lip meant the world to me and you made me laugh with joy!. Rest on daddy, I'm so glad that I got to take care of you, and your medical needs when you were passing away and if I had to do it all over again, I would!. The honor overall, was that I was able to lead you to Jesus Christ, before you closed your eyes, now I know that I will see you again in heaven one day. Your love for me, my sister, our three brothers and your grandchildren was priceless! And grand!. Me and my children enjoyed spending the holidays with you and just being in your presence daddy, we all love you and miss you dearly. Our love for you will be for forever! And more!. This book is dedicated to: My three children, Deondray, Chanyka, Siyia and to my parents, my Mother Betty and my father Charles, may he RIP. Now, To my oldest, elder brother: Dr. David Brown, out in Las Vegas: My brother, David (Aka "Dave") I gave my life over to Christ with you, at the tender age of twelve years young, following your path in Christ as a kid back then. Your life Dave, I followed because I wanted to be just like you serving Jesus Christ faithfully. Thank you, For encouraging me in my many times of need and the trials that I was facing. You gave me hope and pushed me to continue to trust in God's plans for my life. You are truly a good brother and through you, I strive everyday to be a better person and daughter in Christ. You are one of the smartest men that I have ever known and your wisdom and knowledge that you possess is intriguing. Thank you for showing me your strengths and your ability to overcome your own obstacles that you too suffered and overcame in your life, with Christ leading you through. I love you Dave forever and more and thank you! For having my back, praying for me, ministering to me and believing in me. To Maggie: My cousin but, I call you my sister from another mother. We suffered together coming up as kids and adults by family members and relationships not so kind. But, even to this day we have never parted our love for each other, we agree to disagree at times in love. Maggie only me and you know the bond that we will forever share with our children. We both know that we are a phone call or airplane ride away, if need be therefore, I love you sis forever and more. Love you too Sylvester! My cousin's husband.Now, I give thanks to my spiritual family in Christ: Bishop Lonnell Butler, my former Bishop, at the Berean Teaching Center in Gary Indiana. Your fatherly love meant everything to me through my struggles that you supported and ministered me through, with my children for many years, Bishop Butler. Thank you for being there when no one else was, you never once gave up on me as your daughter in Christ, as I served you in the ministry faithfully before God. You will forever have a place in my heart Bishop Butler. To my childhood, former Bishop: Bishop Charles E. Davis RIP, at The Indiana Pentecostal Church of God and Christ, on 35th Indiana, here in Chicago IL. Thank you for standing firm on teaching the true word of God and for helping to lead my soul to Christ at twelve, years young, RIP Bishop Davis. To my sister in Christ and ministry partner for many years, Minister Cheryl Ali, my sister whom I love in Christ. Thank you for helping me when I needed support and you gave without hesitation when you could. Your support throughout the years has been a blessing to me, as I too have been there for you and your mother. May God bless you always, my sister in Christ and thank you all for the ministry that we have shared together as a family and the love that we shared serving together, to all of God's children. Thank you all for your love, phone calls and support through the years. Now, to my long term friends: Michael Stewart, my thirty five year best friend for life. I love you like my brother. We have stood strong! Despite our challenges in life and you Michael, my childhood friend, there will never be a closer friend to me than you have been in my life. Michael, you truly hold a special place in my heart forever. No matter what or how we may disagree at times, God always brings us back together. I love you Michael my special, dear friend for life! And, your mother and siblings. To my friend Barbara Williamsen, my twenty-five year friend for life, the bond we have is forever and thank you for helping me and my children in our times of need, when times got rough for us. I love you dearly and I pray that my support to you over the years was a blessing to you and your daughter as well. Finally, but not least, to my friend Barbara Clark, my seven year buddy and former coworker. We held the hospital down! Over East, here in Chicago working side by side as a team, taking care of sometimes thirty patients at times on our own. We were called "The Head Hunters", by some of the other staff, because when we hit the floor we got the patient care work done! Together. Our conversations over the phone for hours sometimes Barbara Clark helped us to grow, by lifting each other up and encouraging each other day by day and I love you Lady. You have a special place in my heart, your children and your grandchildren as well. All of you here are my true friends that God placed in my life and you all have been with me through the storms and our overcoming from the beginning until now. Thank you! All, for your years of friendships, love, phone calls, visits and conversations of support that helped me, "US" get through the good and bad times. My love for you all is near and never far!. May God continue to bless you all! In his will!. Amen!

About the Author

FIRST, I GIVE all the honor and praise! To my Lord and Savior, Jesus Christ in heaven, for saving my soul and choosing me as his servant and follower. Furthermore, I am a fifty one year young mother born right here in this fabulous city of Chicago IL, residing in the River North community. God has blessed me to be a mother of three beautiful, adult children Deondray, Chanyka and Siyia. I am blessed to have eleven amazing! Grandchildren who are close to my heart. We have an adorable, two year old American Pitbull Terrier named ("Miracle"), My "Spoiled!" Fat! Lil baby girl, who keeps me young and active! More than I want some days (Lol). A few years back, I graduated from Olive Harvey College, Kennedy King College, National Louis University and currently I am attending The Chicago Professional School of Psychology right here in Chicago. In my career, I work as a mental health and substance abuse counselor here in Chicago. Currently, I am finishing my masters degree as a Clinical counselor. Furthermore, my mission as a servant of Christ is to love and serve all ethnicities, races, cultures, gender and ages of God's children and to help lead as many souls to Christ, at one's willingness to serve Christ. I pray that this book that I wrote from my heart, spirit and soul blesses and delivers many of my new readers and friends in many ways. I pray for a better future ahead for you all and that you allow Jesus Christ to close all the negative and traumatic doors of your past. My motto is: Keep! Moving! Forward! And, don't! Look back! Much love to you my new found friends and family!.

Table of Contents

Chapter 1 – A Journey Towards A New Transition To Life-
How It All Began. 1

Chapter 2 – There Is An Old Saying- That Curiosity Killed The Cat. ... 24

Chapter 3 – Love Don't Love Nobody?- But God's Love Is True. 46

Chapter 4 – It's Like Sleeping With The Enemy- Defeat Them
With Your Prayers. 67

Chapter 5 – Sometimes I Feel Like A Crab In A Barrel-
But The Transition Moves Forward. 76

Chapter 6 – Spread Your Wings Like An Eagle- And Fly! High!...... 95

Chapter 7 – Yea, Though I Walk Through The Valley
Of The Shadow Of Death, I Will Fear No Evil!: 116

CHAPTER **1**

A Journey Towards A New Transition To Life- How It All Began.

AS I SIT here on my bed, with my two and, a half year young, Pit Bull Terrier ("Miracle") My fat, lil "Spoiled"! Girl, lying comfortably on her pad, looking at mother dear. Me and, my youngest son, who helps to take care of our puppy, adopted her from the Anti Animal Cruelty Society, on LaSalle here in Chicago, when she was only four or six months young. I have her registered now, as an Emotional Support Animal (ESA), for my son's psychological mental needs and, mine as well. How would I and, my son ever have known that this chucky, active, adorable, big, three year young puppy, would bring so much light into our lives and, home. You will be amazed at how the smallest, the littlest things, in life, you learn to appreciate, over the bigger things, that you thought mattered the most.

I sit here, on the edge of my bed, in the dark at night, in my bedroom, which is my prayer room closet, my quiet time, to unwind and talk to the Lord. I look out from my floor to ceiling, huge window pane windows and, I talk to the stars which are my Angels and, the Lord about any and, everything in my life. My bedroom window outlooks the city of Chicago and, I can see the John Hancock building, not too far away from my sixteen floor window view. Ever since I can remember, at the age of maybe nine years young, the star's way up in the dark, blackish, navy blue sky, they have been my friends and, comfort in my time of need, as I speak to the Lord, for help and guidance.

I can remember looking outside of my bedroom window, as a little girl, with my two older brother's, laying in their twin bed together, in their room, directly across from mine. I would crack the old, dirty sheet that hung as a curtain over my window, to pray to God. And, whenever it rained and thundered, it brought fear to me that the world was coming to an end. I would look for the stars, so I could pray to them, hoping that they would take my prayers up to heaven, to God for me. I would pray and, ask God to please not send me, my parents and, my two brothers to this place "We" Christians and, followers of Jesus Christ, we called this place "Hell". The place that the Bible says, the unrepentant and, non-believers of Jesus Christ, go.

A hot, fiery, death place, with no return to peace, for disobeying the commandments of God and, choosing to live a life of sin. Everytime it thundered and, stormed, I just believed within myself as a child, that the thunder and, lightning sounds meant that God was angry at us. Angry at his children, his creations from the beginning and, he was coming to destroy us all! For our wicked and, evil ways.

I was raised in a Pentecostal COGIC upbringing, where sin and, the book of Revelations were talked about all the time, within our Sunday School lessons, Sunday morning service and, prayer night services. I always felt afraid to do anything wrong, as a child, because I didn't want to displease God and, he judged me, on that great, White Throne Judgement Day, that is sure to come. Even though my parents didn't attend anyone's church, they believed in the word of God and, that Jesus Christ was the son of God.

My parents had no problem with my auntie, my father's sister, who was saved, regularly taking any of the kids in our family to church with her, when she could. I didn't understand the word of God as a child, but I understood right from wrong and, that God hated anything that was evil and, not of him. That much I did understand as a child, from the teachings that I was taught within my family's, church home and, by oher saints, people of God. I remember being twelve years young and, my oldest brother, who was fifteen years young, we both decided to give our life over to Christ.

We were "Tarrying" for the Holy Spirit, they called the Holy Ghost at that time. We tarried with the elders and, the evangelist, the mothers of the church, in the upper rooms of the church, in a small enclosed room, until we spoke in the holy, unknown tongues of Christ. Once the holy spirit and, tongues fell upon me and, my brother, we were both declared delivered and, anointed by the spirit of God then. If you know about Pentecostal COGIC upbringing from the fifties through the eighties, you already know what I mean, when I say, we "Tarried" for the holy spirit and, holy tongues to fall upon us. God has delivered me from these false teachings and, practices within the Church today, Praise God!. You do not have to sit in a room, in a chair, clapping your hands, with the elders coaching you on, with your eyes closed and, repeating Jesus name, over and, over again, until your words start to speak in an unknown language, anymore. Even though I can still, sit with Christ and, speak in these unknown Holy Spirit tongues right now, before the throne of God, in my private prayer to him only, you do not, have to (Tarry) for any holy tongues today!. John 3:16 in the King James Bible says, Vs. 16 For God so loved the world, that he gave his only begotten son, that whosoever believeth in him, should not perish, but have everlasting life!. Amen!

Jesus Christ paid the price at the cross, for all of mankind's sins and, Salvation! Which is free!. Free to all that will accept Jesus Christ as their personal savior and, Lord, turning! Away! From all sins of this world. This is how you receive the holy spirit into your life and, walk holy with Christ, in your everyday life, with your family as well. There are no rituals! As to how to receive the holy spirit of God!.

In my upbringing within the Pentecostal church teachings, they were called at that time of my deliverance to Christ, the Holy! Rollers! The Saints of God, who served in the Pentecostal COGIC denomination way back then. It was a very strict way of living, very, legalistic within our church beliefs. The women or teenage girls could not wear any form of makeup, no jewelry, colored nail polish, big earrings, open toed or heeled dress shoes, no skirts over the knees.and, no fake, long hair. And, the women and, girls were forbidden! From wearing pants period! Inside or outside of the church!. Men were considered the only ones who could wear pants and, shorts, not the girls or women.

Therefore, I was "Groomed"! Along with my brother well, by the Saints of God, about living a holy, committed and, dedicated lifestyle to Jesus Christ in heaven. Wow! Those were some rough, hard and, trying times back then. I really didn't have an understanding of the word of God for myself and, being told by the elders of the church that the way you dressed and, your appearance could send you to hell! Which I know today, is absolutely not true!. I know today, from my own studies of the word of God, in my fifties now, that those were all man made rules and, has nothing! To do with your personal relationship with Christ. It was hard for me being a young, shy, insecure, introverted, twelve year old child in grammar school, trying to live up to the expectations of the church beliefs and, not God's beliefs.

I didn't understand why at twelve years young, I was told by my auntie and, the Saints of God, that we could not wear pants once we were saved in Christ. I wondered what did a girl or woman wearing pants have to do with your salvation in the Lord?. Even in the winter time, we had to wear skirts and, dresses, so, we would wear these thick, wool like tights underneath our skirts and, dresses. Or we wore legging pants underneath our skirts and, dresses to keep our legs from freezing while walking outside. I had to walk ten blocks, to get to school, with my two, older brothers, with gym shoes or boots on. My coat only came to my hips, so I practically froze! In the winter, walking five days a week, there and, back from school in these dresses and, skirts, in ten to twelve inches of snow, in Chicago's winter, when we walked to school. I dared not! Wear any girl's pants! And, be out of the will of God!. That's what the women of the church hammered! Into our heads, that only disobedient, children of God, dressed this way and, we would be punished! By God. I am so over! Tradition! And, the legalistic behavior, within some of the Churches today, which is a form of control! And, bondage! That only cripples! The church and, its people today!.

Whoever decided to make it a law, that women can only wear skirts and, dresses, no makeup, jewelry, nail polish, or fake hair, in this century of time, can't be realistic themselves at all. We are not under the law! In the Bible today, but grace! We are under God's grace today and, women can wear pants, a little makeup and, hair, to make themselves feel good. It is not written in God's commandments, that a woman wearing pants, makeup and, hair will be doomed! To hell! For doing so. I think it's the soul of a person that we should be more worried about, not so much as to, what a person is wearing to church?. As long as we are wearing our clothes as young and, older people in decency and, in order, to not distract others from the word of God, I see nothing wrong with adding to your appearance, to help boost your self-esteem if needed, about yourself. As people of God, many of us, we sometimes focus on the wrong things within the Church, why don't we focus more on teaching the word of God, sharing the good news of God and, helping those who are in need, instead of casting! People to hell! Because of how they may dress or look. God's word has its way of cleaning people up, in his timing and, will, no one gave us the gavel! As, the dress code! Enforcer!. Let's get people in the church who need Christ and, let God's word penetrate their hearts and, deal with them in his perfect timing and, will to do so, towards their own will to change.

All the kids in my grammar school thought I was going to become some type of "Nun" one-day and, they thought I was special, (Not in a good way, either) for committing to my church values at my age. I was just doing what I was told Christian girls and, women do and, that's to be totally different, with my behavior and, ways than those who lived a life in sin. For a twelve year old, there were just things about Christianity that a young child my age could not fully comprehend, as an adult in their Christian life, could understand.

I remember I tried out for the cheerleader team, to boost my low self-esteem about myself. All the pretty girls, that the boys liked, were on the cheerleader team. The girls were either light skinned, with long pretty hair and, had nice figures for their age. I was not light skinned, I was a caramel complexion and, I did not have long hair. My hair was medium length, just past my neck and, my mother had to hot, comb it regularly, in order to get my hair straight, from the coarse, four C hair that I had and, my lil sister too. I wasn't gorgeous like most of the girls were, but I was cute to look at, with a normal, cute face, and, skinny, frail body like a stick. I never would have believed in a million years that I would make the cheerleader team. But, I actually made it on the cheerleader team, after tryouts, because I could do a perfect split and, I could hold my arms stiff and, straight as a board, with the pom-pom's.

If a girl could do a split and, keep her arms tight and, stiff you automatically made the team. I was so happy to get on the cheerleader team, I could not believe they let me on the team and, surprisingly, none of the girls made fun of me and, that was a shock! All by itself. They actually welcomed me to the team. But, would you believe, the church members said girls could not join the cheerleader team, because the skirts came up to your butt, and, your thighs could not be out, as a Christian girl. So, after one week on the team, learning the routines, I was told I had to quit the team, by the members of the church and, my Holy! Roller! Auntie.

There goes my self-esteem! Right back out of the window!. This church stuff was really getting on my nerves, no pants, no cheerleader team and, there were certain cartoons that we couldn't watch, because there was a lot of violence within the cartoons, the church leaders said. They didn't want us to watch "Popeye"! Because the church folks said, he and, "Bluto"! Were fighting each other over a woman, which was " Olive Oyl" and, that was a form of abuse and, sexism concerning women. That does makes sense today, to monitor what your children are watching on television, but, can you believe back in the 70s, 80s and, 90s how traditional and, legalistic some of the churches were, with some of their man made beliefs?.

Sometimes all the rules of the can'ts and, don'ts can take away from the true messages of God. It is so important for the leaders of the church to just preach and, teach the word of God, as it is written. God's word does not need anything added to it by man or anything taken away from God's word either. If you are accurately teaching the word of God, the word of God will go out and, do what it is supposed to do, to touch the hearts of people, on its own, God's word can stand alone for itself!. There are too many leaders, who are preaching from their personal feelings and, not enough about the word of God. My belief is, if you allow the word of God to dwell within you fully, whatever changes that need to be made about you, the word of God has its way of convicting us and, allowing us, to make the changes that we need, In God's timing, not man's. I had a heavy! Cross to carry, at only eleven or twelve years young, going to school, trying to fulfill all of these Christian beliefs.

I always took my Bible to school and, I never wore pants, only dresses and, skirts outside the house. The other kids my age didn't have an understanding about the Lord, living holy and, staying away from sinful ways and, behaviors. All they wanted to know was why you were the way that you were?. I was taunted at times, made fun of and, called crazy! By some of the other kids, because of my personal belief in the word and, ways of God that I tried, so hard to live out. Can you imagine how heavy of a cross that was for me to carry everyday as a twelve year young girl, not even understanding who I was, as a kid, let alone a Christian?. As I continued to pray to God, as a kid and, believing in the word of God, I managed to push my way, through the many situations that I faced, throughout my childhood and, adult life.

God says, in his word in, John Ch.15 Vs. 20 it reads, Remember the word that I said unto you, the servant is not greater than his lord. If they have persecuted me, they will also persecute you; if they have kept my saying, they will keep yours also. Amen!

Jesus Christ, was made the sacrificial lamb and, he himself was abused, hit, beaten, whipped, spit upon, falsely accused, and, nailed to the cross of Calvary, all for mankind's sins and, murdered!. If Jesus

Christ had to pay the price for our sins, then why not, you ("Me") be betrayed, let down, hurt, lied on, mistreated and, abandoned by family members, spouses, associates and, friends?. None of us are exempt from life's challenges, that will happen to us all, at times.

There is no easy way to this life, that we are a part of here on earth, situations will happen and, problems will occur, that will be out of our will and, control at times. But, there is a road map to life that Christ prophets wrote and, left behind for us to read, study, absorb, memorize and, apply to our lives, daily.

That road map is the Holy Bible, which is the word of God, and, guidance for our lives, our problems, careers, goals, family, marriage, spirit and, soul!. Just think about it, if we all could just take the time to apply a lot of the scriptures to our lives, consulting with God first, before we make any decisions and, choices first, half of the problems and, struggles that we experience could be avoided. Many of us are so quick! To rely on the promises of people and, this world's system, that is clearly failing! Us! Everyday it seems. Lord, knows that a lot of the problems that I too have today, is because, I trusted more in this world's corrupted system and, man, over trusting in the will of God for my life. Today, I am focused on rewriting some of my wrongs and, moving forward! As, I trust God first, to guide and, lead me through. Can we start over fresh, from our past mistakes? Yes we can, with hard work and, commitment towards change, for our good.

Today in my life, at fifty, one years young, I am restarting my life over again and, asking myself some serious questions, about where it all started for me? And, where am I in my life today?. I am petitioning God, in my daily prayers, to show me who I am? Where art thou? And, what is it that God wants me to do, for God's kingdom purposes, here on earth?. It is not too late for any of us to start all over again from scratch, go back to the basics and, revisit Genesis, the beginning of God's creations. Sometimes it may require you to revisit your past mistakes and, focus on the work, to create a more positive outlook for your life and, family. It may require a period of isolation for your healing, forgiveness of those who hurt us, discipline, commitment, balance, prayer and, time with God. But, it can be done! Change is possible, if you want it bad enough!.

Today, as you read along with me here, my new friends and, family, I am going to share with all of you, how my life started, from an abused baby in my mother's womb, the trauma that I have suffered, from people, family members and, within two, marriages that I was forced to walk away from, due to abuse and, infidelity. This is my roadmap to recovery with Christ today. A lot of the messages, teachings and, wisdom that I will be sharing with you, my readers, is to help lead you towards your own healing, prayerfully to help deliver and, lead those to Christ, who are out of the will of God and, for you to establish a much, closer relationship with God, at your own will, to do so.

My journeys are to help those who have experienced any forms of traumatic emotional, physical, mental or spiritual abuse, that I too, have suffered in my past and, I am still doing the work with Christ, towards my healing today. My stories of my life are up close in your face, raw and, deep! Therefore, brace yourself for my 100% authentic truth!. I have quite a few stories to share with you about the many trials and, tribulations that I have suffered. I will share with you why I am starting my life back over, with God as head of my life and, guiding my paths along the way. I will be using many, powerful! scriptures of the Holy Bible (KJV) as well, that God gave me within my spirit, to help strengthen you, as food for your soul! And, wisdom from the word of God!.

Take a ride with me, back down memory lane, as I begin the journey of my life. Let's move forward!. Amen!

I sit here, looking outside of my bedroom window, at fifty one, years young and, I ask myself, where am I at, in my life today? And, I often ask myself how did I get here, through the obstacles that I have faced from my childhood, through today?.

I call out to Christ in my weariness, in the midnight hours, because I want God to come find me and, see about me. There are a lot of times when I am feeling afraid, lost in a life of chaos, hurt and, betrayals by others and, I want God to, call out my name and, ask me, "Where Art Thou"!?.

In the book of Genesis Ch 3 Vs. 8 Th.10 it reads, And, they heard the voice of the LORD God walking in the garden in the cool of the day: and Adam and his wife hid themselves from the presence of the LORD God amongst the trees of the Garden. V. 9 And the LORD God called unto Adam, and said unto him, Where art thou?. V. 10 And he said, I heard the voice in the garden, and I was afraid, because I was naked; and hid myself. Amen!

In my times of being isolated with God, I pray daily, asking and, hoping for the Lord at times, to call out my name in my time of needs or downfalls. I welcome the voice of God, to walk, in the garden and, pastures, asking me why am I hiding my face from him? And, "Where Art Thou"!?.

I know there are a lot of people who would disagree and, say, oh! No! I don't want the Lord to call out my name and, seek me that way, because it means that you have done something wrong and, God is going to punish you! For it. Well, I can dig it and, to some degree, depending on the circumstances that may be true. But, I have my own stance and, different thoughts about this, on my own behalf.

When I look at the condition of many of my family members, associates, people I know or see, who are suffering and, many of them, don't have a personal relationship with Christ and, are living in a life of despair.

I look at many of the different races and, ethnicities of people across this world, who are living in poverty, homelessness, addicted to drugs, pills or alcohol. Many are suffering from mental health illnesses, and, like myself, have experienced some form of physical, emotional and, mental abuse at the hands of others. There are many people, even myself because of my skin color, who have been racially discriminated against, because of their norms of life, culture, gender, their spiritual beliefs and, choices. There are people who have lost everything, as I too have experienced multiple times, losses of finances, our place to live, careers, jobs, marriages, health and, the death of our loved ones.

We see the corruption within our hierarchical governments, healthcare systems, judicial systems and, the poison from the music industry, plays a part in the wickedness as well of this world. Even the demonic, music videos that spew out hate, wickedness, evilness, sex, drugs, murder, and, satanic satanism worship. And, the occult brainwashing of some of our women, men, boys and girls, who are being pulled into these satanic lifestyles. There are thousands of young and, older women and, men who are being sex trafficked across the world. The list of sinful, evilness within the people today, goes on and, on, within our society, communities, families, church, jobs and, across the world today.

This wicked system has made it where everything that is good and, pleasing to God is bad and, everything that is wicked and, of Satan is now considered good!. So, many people fail to see or acknowledge that this evilness and, wickedness is far more deeper than I and, you will ever imagine. There is a true demonic force! That is responsible for the destructive behavior of evil and, wicked people. These wicked forces are destroying families, communities and, causing the wars of people against each other, with the mass killing of innocent children and, adults across the world. The enemy controls the winds that cause tornadoes, hurricanes and, earthquakes with unexpected and, devastating destruction! And, lives lost in its aftermath of effects. We have witnessed all of this that I am talking about through our news, talk radio and, social media platforms that keep us informed about what is happening across the world.

If you read, Ephesians Ch. 6 Vs.12, we will find the answer's, as to what we are really fighting against, on this earth and in the spiritual rhymes and it reads, Vs. 12 For we wrestle not against flesh and blood, but against principalities, against powers, against the rulers of the darkness of this world, against spiritual wickedness in high places. Amen!

These are the evil, spiritual powers that are dividing people of all races, many church leaders, perishoners, dividing marriages, destroying many through their health, we have nations against nations and, so much more. We are wrestling as the scriptures says, against principalities, against powers, against the rulers of the darkness of this world, spiritual wickedness in high places!. These are the strong, powerful, demonic, satanic force's! That are taking over the lives of many of our people, many nations and, governments today.

There are so many people who are being used by these wicked spirit's and, dark, powerful! forces! To do evil works! Of Satan and, his adversaries today. We ourselves do not have the power to fight Satan and, his foot soldiers on our own, no we do not!. But, we have the Holy Scriptures and, the Holy Spirit within us, to fight! Against! The enemies' plans and, attacks against us and, our loved ones. Therefore, our super! Weapon! That we have, against the enemy is God! Almighty! Who has the power over all! Evil works of mankind, by Satan and, his adversaries against us.

We, who are submitted to the will of God, we thank God for choosing us, to be his soldiers and, children unto him. We have a 24 hour a day, 365 days of the year, prayer line, to call out the name of Jesus Christ! For help! In our time of need. We can cry out for God, to come and, see about us and, God will answer! His children's prayers. All we have to do, is believe! And, trust God to strengthen us, through our issues that we may face. God is our protection and, defense against the attacks of the enemy, against our lives. Trust the process and, timing, but, please don't allow the enemy to cause you to lose your faith, because of the circumstances that you may be facing. Amen!

There have been so many, dark moments throughout my life, even now and, I suffered for many years fighting depression, anxiety, panic attacks and, PTSD from my past traumatic experiences. There were many moments in my life, where I didn't think that I could go on, in the despair and, the pain that I was in for years, on. I couldn't go to family members who never accepted me or cared about me and, the people who were around me, many of them, were just as broken! As I was. They had their own, personal struggles that they were facing too. It was my tears to God and, crying out to him, in my weakest moments, for me to get through the pains and, trauma that I was suffering from. It's something about that name Jesus! That always got me through, each time that I wanted to give up, roll over and, die!. That sweet, name of Jesus Christ, God always called out to me, just when I needed to hear God's voice the most and, God called out to my spirit, Where Art Thou!?. I didn't know myself where I was and, where my life was going, but I trusted the presence of God in my life, to guide me and, to carry me through. When you get to the point in your life, where you feel like you have no one by your side, your life has been turned upside-down, call out to God! In those moments of trials that you are facing. God will help you to get through it, in his perfect timing and, will. Just remember that God is waiting right there for us, to call him to rescue us, even sometimes, from ourselves.

We don't have to do a chant, or pray five to seven times a day, like a ritual, to get God's attention, no, we don't. We don't have to pray to any statues or confess our sins to a man, to get God's attention and, forgiveness, no, we don't!. As children of God, all we have to do is turn from the sins of this world, repent for our sins, confess God to be the son of God and, believe that God died and, rose on the third day. Once you (We) have accepted Jesus Christ as our personal Lord and, Savior, we are now welcomed! Into the kingdom of God and, God's holy spirit dwells within us!. Amen!

Our name is written in God's book of life forever! And, no man, woman, boy, girl or demon! From hell! Can pluck! You (Us) from the hands of God!. It reads in the scriptures in, John Ch.10 Vs. 27 Th 29 it reads, My sheep hear my voice, and I know them, and they follow me:[28] And I give unto them eternal life; and they shall never perish, neither shall any man pluck them out of my hand.[29] My Father, which gave them me, is greater than all; and no man is able to pluck them out of my Father's hand. Amen!

When the Rapture occurs, the saints will be Raptured up! With God. You do not! Want to be still here, left on earth, during the seven years of tribulation that occurs. It says, in the scriptures in, 1 Thessalonians Ch. 4 Vs. 16-17 it reads, [16] For the Lord himself shall descend from heaven with a shout, with the voice of the archangel, and with the trump of God: and the dead in Christ shall rise first:[17] Then we which are alive and remain shall be caught up together with them in the clouds, to meet the Lord in the air: and so shall we ever be with the Lord. Amen!

During the seven year tribulation, it's going to feel like death! On earth! There will be people in pain, unbelievable suffering! Sorrow, crying, murder, starvation and, worst more!. Destruction! Will be all across this world! People will suffer enslavement from the anti Christ and, there will be unthinkable things! Disasters to occur!. You can read in the book of Revelations Ch.19 for more about what happens during the seven year tribulation when the Lord returns for the judgment. And, as I said, you do not want to be left behind during that time, need I say more?. I pray that the imaginary lightbulb, above your head, has come on here.

In my time of need, when I am struggling in my faith, weary from the blows and, constant attacks on my life, who do I go to for help? And, who do I trust and cry out to?. Yes! The one that I want to come and, see about me, is none other than the Lord, my savior and, my everything! Jesus Christ.

Let us try to understand that there is forgiveness and, comfort in the arms of the Lord. Yes, God will chastise us at times in our lives, but, isn't that what a loving and, concerned parent does?. When they see that you need a bit of redirecting, when it seems that you have gotten off the path, somehow? It is only for your good, not to harm you, but to protect you from the harmful things that we cannot at times, see with our own instincts. With God, you (We) get the chance to ask God for forgiveness, turn from those sins and, God will pick us up, dust us off, wipe our tears and, start us back again on our way!. What a amazing! God, that we serve, that will give us countless chances to get it right. People's love will fail you, let you down but, God's love for us all, is unconditional and, can never! Fail any of us. For these reasons, to God! I give him all! The praise!.

I think many of us underestimate the power and, love that God has for us, his children. Our God is almighty! All powerful! And,

Omni-present! Meaning, that God can be everywhere, at the same time, all over this world!. Satan, does not have the power, to be everywhere at the same time, as God, he is not almighty, nor all powerful over the Lord, no. God is God! And, there is no other name, above his name, God is the ruler! Over all! Nations! Kingdoms! And, Governments here on earth. God is the only God that died and, Rose! On the third day! There was none! Before God and, there will be none! After God! Can I get an Amen!. God's love for (Us) his children is everlasting! And, people at times, will turn their love, on and, off to us, like a light switch, when we do something that they don't agree with or to punish you, for their own personal justification. God's love is everlasting and, he gives us, chance after chance to get back aligned, in his will, for our lives. I used to hear older folks say, when I was a kid, I'm so glad that people don't have a heaven! Or hell! To cast me in, because if they could, I would have been gone a long! Time ago! At their judgments and, convictions of me. At my age today, I understand that saying so, well to be true, by others, with their suspicious looks and, assumptions of others.

For many years of my life, even today, I have been accused of things that I didn't do. I have been lied on, misunderstood, judged by cousins, relatives, siblings, also within two, horrible! Marriages and, by associates, with these wrongful accusations, without real cause!?. Thank you Lord! That you know our hearts, you knew us before we were even born and, I am grateful! That I owe no one! Any explanation about who I am In Christ, as God's chosen servant! And, it is only what God knows of me that counts!. Don't spend any of your time trying to prove yourself to those who may never accept you for who you truly are, it is a waste of your time and energy!. Many of these people are not happy with how their own lives are and, many of them may even be jealous and, envious of the life that you have created for yourself. Furthermore, some people just won't like you, no matter what you may do and, it's okay, people are who they are and, it is not our job to change them. Pray for these people and, relatives who are really broken themselves and, need to seek Christ for their own healing. The only person that we can change and, save is ourselves! Give these people, family members, associates, whomever, over to Christ, close the doors to them, wash your hands to them, moving! Forward! And, don't! Look! Back!. Our change begins within ourselves and, not others, the work must begin within you!.

It is not too late to start over fresh, get back in the will of God right now, by rejuvenating your life, plans and, goals. Don't do it later, because the next few seconds or days are not promised, for any of us, to still be breathing, so, why not make the changes right now!?. Who cares about what people may think, say, or perceive you to be, their opinions of you or about you, it's not of your concern. You (We) have bigger! Fish to fry! Than sitting around worrying about the small minded, "Mino Fish" in the bottom of the bait bucket!. Hello! Are you awakening to some clarity about your life now?. I pray that I am opening your wisdom further and, understanding concerning this thing called life. And, the possibilities that we have right now, to start a fresh change in your life and, spirit today. Amen! Let me continue on here.

What I have learned about people, family, friends or associates, is that people will forever! Remember your wrongs or downfalls in your life. But, they will hardly acknowledge the good works! That you have done, to make changes, to right some of your wrongs!. Some people will forgive you and, give you another chance, yes, but there are the ones who will cast! You to Hell! If they could without a trial!.

Then, you have the ones who will say that they forgive you and, love you, but they will always be watching you, with that third, silent, side eye, all the time!. Hello! I know from experience of dealing with these types of family members and, associates. That's why I can say these things out loud, because I have witnessed the betrayals and, seen it all, hand in hand. If I want anyone to chastise me for my wrongs and, bad decisions that I myself have made in life, I would rather, it be by God himself and, not from people!. At least I would receive a true and, honest trial without malice, and, given the opportunity to get back aligned with Christ. Some of the challenges that I have endured in my life from the attacks of others and, myself, have been long, suffering and, life altering in many good and, bad ways.

I ask myself sometimes, when did my pain and, suffering begin? And, how did I get to this season of rejuvenation, purification, isolation and, starting my life over, at Fifty-one years young?. I remember this is how it began.

As far as I can remember, I have always throughout my life, infancy, toddler, preschool, early school years, adolescent years, young adulthood and middle adulthood, have experienced some form of trauma or abuse in my life, as I researched Erik Erikson's theory, his hypothesis covers eight life stages of life. When you get a chance, google his name, and, take a look at some of his theories, it's an interesting read.

Deep within my mother's womb, I was abused from my mother's womb, yes, I said, I was abused from my mother's womb. My dear, sweet little mother, who is about seventy one today, was twenty years young, when she bore me into this world called life. My mother is one of the strongest, loving, caring and, most loyal women that I will ever know. I know, your question to me is, how were you abused from the womb?. Okay, I will further explain my point. My father, God rest his soul, he passed away at the young age of sixty four years young, from fourth stage lung cancer. When we found out, the cancer had already spread to all of his major organs and, even in the bones of his left thigh, when he was diagnosed with cancer.

My father and, mother were both raised in the backwoods, of the Jim Crow days and, horrible! Segregation times, in Philadelphia Mississippi as children, with their parents, relatives and, siblings. My father and, some of his siblings couldn't go to school beyond elementary school. My father had to sharecrop, pick cotton and, work hard labor to survive with my grandmother. Furthermore, my father and, mother witnessed a lot of horrible things! Things that were inhumane and, unjustly done to his family and, Blacks as young kids, that no child or adult should have ever experienced.

My father also started drinking moonshine, (Alcohol) smoking cigars and, cigarettes as a young kid, he told me, during one of our many conversations about his life, in Philadelphia Mississippi. They migrated to Chicago's South Side for a new beginning of life in the late 60s, but, unfortunately, my father was already addicted to alcohol and, tabaco, before they left Mississippi. My poor, little, five, feet four mother, took a lot of physical beatings, mental and, emotional abuse at the hands of my father, throughout their twenty something years of marriage, before separating, not divorcing.

Many years later in life, my father left my mother around the time that me and, my four siblings were young adults. So, as I said, my mother also suffered physical abuse during her pregnancies with my father. Therefore the pain and, emotional abuse that my mother suffered, while carrying me, I "too!" felt that abuse, from within her womb!. All the emotional trauma that my mother was experiencing, from my father's abuse towards her, during those nine months of my conception was real!. I came out of my mother's womb, already, experiencing physical abuse, at the hands of my own father!. There are a lot of babies that have been born, with physical handicaps to their bodies, even brain damage, from the mother being physically beaten, by either the father of the child, a relative or someone that she trusted, to be close to her. There have been babies born, still born, (Not alive) due to some form of abuse that happened to the mother, while she was carrying the child. Therefore, a child can already be physically abused, from the womb of the mother, before the child is even born! And, as I said, I was a victim of physical abuse, before my mother had even conceived me into the world and the term is called medically (IPU) intimate partner violence and can have a range of negative impacts on both the pregnant person and the developing fetus. This negative effect can carry through into childhood and beyond.

Many years later, in my forties, I thank God today that I was the one who cared for my father, the last year before he passed away and, I was able to lead his soul to Christ, before he closed his eyes. To God! I give him all! The Praise!. There are many people that don't understand that whatever the mother experiences, during the time that she carries, that baby in her womb, whether it be emotions of joy, happiness, pain, sadness, or physical abuse, it can be detrimental to the quality of life that the child may have, mentally or physically once they are born!.

For instance, if a mother drinks a large consumption, regularly of alcohol drinks, consume any type of drugs, pharmaceutical or street pills or she may smoke cigarettes, while carrying a baby, there is a high chance, that the baby may be born with severe life altering, health issues, physical deformities, or born with with, Fetal Alcohol Spectrum Disorders (FASDs). What you feed, swallow, inhale, inject or pollute into your body, that is unhealthy while carrying a baby in your womb, can cause that baby a lifetime of severe health issues, even premature death! At birth. Need I say more?. I pray that you are learning a lot from the information that I share with you. Take the time to do your own research on some of these topics to further educate yourself as well, knowledge is power! And, food!.

I have always felt, in some ways, that the trauma, that I experienced from my mother's womb affected me in many ways as a child, who was always afraid, fearful and, timid growing up. Let me express this as well, this is not a form of any generational curse! But, an abusive pattern or cycle that I could not explain or understand as a child. There are no! Generational curses! To those who believe in generational curses. Jesus Christ died on the Cross of Calvary, for all! Of mankind's sins! And, all curses were broken! Destroyed! At the Cross!. Therefore, because Christ paid the price for mankind's sins, there are no curses! Today! Praise! God!. There are no soul! Ties! Either, no one can tie themselves to another person's soul, this is foolery! False doctrine! And, not biblical at all!. Get under a good, sound, Bible teaching leader, that can teach you and, guide you through the word of God, to know these things for yourself. The Bible says, in 2 Timothy Ch. 2 Vs. 15 it reads, Study to show thyself approved unto God, a workman that needeth not to be ashamed, rightly dividing the word of truth. Amen!. If somebody tells you something that doesn't align with you, go and, do the research always for yourself! Amen!.

My first traumatic experience happened when I was two or four years young. We lived in this thirty unit old, gray, stone brick, apartment building that had these tall, radiator gas heaters that burned inside with fire, to heat up your house. The radiator had an exhaust pipe that went up through the wall, through a vent, to carry out the smoke and, toxic fumes. The problem with these types of radiator heaters back in the seventies, was that they stood about as tall as your hip area and, they were made of steel or metal. You could see the fire from the front vent, burning inside.

There was no protective covering around it, to protect you or your children from burns, if you touched it or fell into it. These gas radiators were a serious health and, safety hazard for breathing in these harmful fumes, as well. It was against the law for landlords to have these types of radiator heaters set up, to warm their buildings, without a protective covering around it, for the safety of their tenants. My mother somehow, one-day, while my father was at work, took her eyes off of me for a short while, leaving me on the coach, near the gas radiator heater. And, I had somehow jumped from the coach, jumping, they said and, landed face, stomach, arm and, leg down, on top of the scorching! Hot! Steal heater!.

My mother recalls hearing the terror! Of my screams, she ran back to the front room, having to pull me off of the heater. Most of my flesh pulled off, as my mother pulled me off the radiator, as my flesh was cooking like meat, on the top of the metal heater. This was one of the worst! Situations of my mother, father, his mother and, siblings life at that time. I had third and, fourth degree burns to my forehead, the left side of my lower stomach, my left inner thigh and, left forearm. My mother and, father said I spent months in the burn unit and, in intensive care. Not to forget, DCFS and, the police were called on my mother to start their own investigation as to how I fell upon the radiator heater, without my mother being present.

The state was conducting an active child neglect and, endangerment case against my mother that lasted for about a year, or so, I was told. Everything had to be presented through the courts, in order for my mother to be proven innocent of child neglect and, child endangerment charges, at my mother's own hands. I thank God! That he covered my mother from those charges, that could have landed her in prison for many years, leaving my two, oldest brothers behind, without a mother to care for them. Also, with the help of my father, his mother and, sisters at that time, who were working diligently with my parents through the court hearings. They all were traveling, back and, forth to the hospital, to spend time with me and, to court, pleading on my mother's behalf, that she did not have anything to do, with me being severely burned, nearly death intentionally, at my mother's hands.

When I think about it today, the trauma that I, as a toddler went through and, all of the tremendous pains that I had to have endured, from the burns all over my little body. My little body, laying on top of that scorching! Hot! Metal radiator and, my skin being pulled! Off! As, my poor mother had to snatch! Me up! From the radiator to save me, from further burns!. My poor mother and, father, at that time, the torture! That they had to endure, from the false! Accusations of some of my father's family members, the courts and, others against them. I can only imagine my parents sitting at my bedside day and, night looking down at their baby girl, severely! Burned all over. My parents sat with me everyday and, every night for months at a time, praying to God for my life and, my healing. They withered through that storm, until it all eventually came to an end, with the courts and DCFS. In due time, God healed my badly burned body, as I was released back to my parents again. All! Praise! Be unto God! Amen!.

As of today, you can't even see a mark on my forehead or face and, the burn on my left arm, left side of my stomach and, left leg is still there, but, not as bad looking, to the sight anymore, from way back then. Praise God! He is a healer my poor, dear mother's name, was cleared of any wrongful doing. But, of course, some of those family members of my father's never cleared my mother's name, with their viciousness! Lies and, slander! About my mother. But, who cares! God cleared my mother's name! And, that's all that matters today. Amen!.

Have you ever been put into a situation in your life by people, friends or family who have falsely accused you of something that you know you did not say or do?. I'm sure many of you have, where you have had to fight! For your character and, name to prove your innocence, from those who set out traps to destroy you!. It's not a good feeling, when the very people that you loved or trusted turned their backs on you, used you, hurt you, lied on you, abandoned you, and, betrayed your heart. It hurts! Because we have emotions and, feelings as human beings, we all cry at times from pain and, grief in our lives.

Remember, God warned us in his holy word, in the scriptures, that false accusations against you (Us) would come and, we would in fact be persecuted for his name's sake as well. In Matthew Ch. 5 Vs. 11-12 it reads, Blessed are ye, when men shall revile you, and persecute you, and shall say all manner of evil against you falsely, for my sake. V. 12 Rejoice, and be exceedingly glad: for great is your reward in heaven: for so persecuted they the prophets which were before you. Amen!

Jesus' 12 disciples, the Apostles of Christ, some were beaten, mocked by the people, falsely accused, mistreated, lied upon and, not welcomed by many of the people. Jesus was hated by these false prophets, false religious leaders, the Pharisees and, Saudeucess for his teaching of his father, to the lost, enslaved and, abused. Jesus Christ himself, was even imprisoned, brutally beaten! Nailed to a cross and, killed! By his own people!. All for mankind's sins and, for our salvation!. Amen!. We all have a free will, to choose right or wrong, but, one thing about it is, you cannot partake of both! Lifestyles, no!. We are to be as followers of Christ's examples, we cannot partake of the sinful ways of this ungodly! World of many people. We have to choose whose side will you follow? Good or bad? And, there is only one right way, that is total surrenderance, repentance, unto the will of God!. There is no other way. Amen!.

I'd rather lose my soul to Christ, than lose my soul participating in the sinful ways and, wickedness of this world's ungodly system.

To those who willingly choose to live in a life of sin, trust me here, it will cost you, your life, even at times your family, your loved ones, your health, your career, your finances, job and, more!. We cannot win, when it comes to the ruler of this world, the principalities and, powers of this world! Without Christ in our lives. You just don't have that kind of human power, alone to defeat the enemy and, his satanic tactics against your life, we don't. But, we can have an everlasting life, in Christ, in heaven, without any price to pay and, with Christ in your life, you will never! Lose!. God fights the enemy for us! He has the power! Over the enemy and, as we should know, Satan has already lost! The battle!. He has already been defeated!. And, on judgment day, he, his adversaries, all the false Prophets, Hell! Along with all the non-believers of Christ, will be cast! Into the Lake of Fire! For eternity! By God!. We win! As believers and, followers of Christ, in the end! Amen!. I pray that this is a headliner moment, an eye opener moment, for my readers. We have already Won! The victory! As believers of Christ and, we have permanent! Residency in heaven! With the Lord! When the rapture of the saints of God, soon occurs. Need I say more?. Amen!. Okay, let's move on further, I still have so, much to share.

CHAPTER **2**

There Is An Old Saying-
That Curiosity Killed The Cat.

I CAN REMEMBER one night, while me, my two brothers and, parent's were sleeping in our beds, we heard some gunshots right by this big, vacant, parking lot next to our thirty unit building. It was during a cold winter, snowy month and, the big, vacant lot was covered with hard, slippery snow. My mother had wrapped me up like a snowman the next day and, she was walking me this early morning to school, because my brothers had already left for school. I was around nine years old and, a curious little girl. As we were walking past the vacant lot, I looked over and, I saw something far off, in the middle of the snow, it was red blood stains. I asked my mother, was that spot, from the man that the neighbors said was shot and, killed there last night?. The whole building of neighbors were talking about it to each other that morning, as word had spread about the shooting.

My mother looked over at the spot, curious herself and, answered, I don't know?. Out of my curiosity, I asked her if I could go and, see the spot and, my mother, for some reason, said very quickly, yes. She stood, as I anxiously ran over, seeing the bright, red blood stains in the snow. Out of my fear, from seeing the blood, I slid down, falling, almost unto the blood!. Out of terror! I began to cry, screaming! And, calling out! for my mother, as I scrambled to get up from the cold and, hard snow. I screamed out to her, to come! And, see about me! But, instead, I could hear my mother laughing at me and, yelling for me to come back! To her. I ran as fast as I could, terrified! As I grabbed for my mother's hand, at relief, as she held onto me, dusting the snow off my snowsuit that I had on.

My mother looked down at me, as I was crying, and she told me, "That's what I get, for being so nosey! And, wanting to look at something, that had nothing to do with me". In other words, in her own way, she was teaching me a lesson about staying away from things that could be harmful or dangerous to my wellbeing. She was teaching me at that moment, that when you walk away from the very thing that is there to protect you, it can cause you great harm, in the aftermath of the consequences of your actions, then or later!. I held on to my mother's hand so tightly, as she embraced me, she made me feel so, much more protected and, secured, as we walked away from that lot. All I could think was, some poor soul, lost his life, for some reason, in that very spot, that I slid down in, out of my mother's will!. Do you get what I am saying here?. Sometimes we too, can put our own selves, in a position to be harmed, by the wrong decisions and, choices that we make, outside of the will of God!. It's not always about the devil did this and, the devil did that or the devil is busy! No!. Sometimes the problem and, the enemy can be us!. Amen!. We have to learn, to take full accountability, for some of the situations and, things that we did to harm ourselves, even our families. And, some of the bad things, that we allowed people to continue to do, to harm us, when we should have let them go! The first time that people wronged us. Sometimes we just have to reevaluate our own thinking and, do some work within ourselves. Even if it takes you, going to get some counseling or seeking psychological help, by medical professionals, as I too, have done for many years now for my own healing and, medical treatment. There is nothing wrong with reaching out to get the proper medical help that you may need, for your own healing. I have been receiving psychological help and, prescription treatment through my psychiatrist and, medical doctors, for the last ten years so far. The best thing that I could ever do, for myself, was when I finally decided that it was time for me to seek further help, for my psychological traumas, that I didn't have a diagnosis for, for over thirty five years of my life. Prayer is always good for anyone. But, when it comes down to your mental and, physical health, you should seek a medical professional, to help you figure out things about your health, get the proper diagnosis and, treatment that can help you with your physical and, emotional needs. Okay, let me get back to the story at hand.

Right at that moment, when I fell down, next to some poor guys, last demise and, bloody fluids, I experienced my "third" traumatic experience, since being born from my mother's womb. "First" from the trauma in my mother's womb of physical abuse, "Second" from nearly dying, at two or four years old, from third and, fourth degree burns, all over my little, body and, "Thirdly" from my curiosity, of wanting to go see, what had happened to some poor, man's life and, sliding down in the victim's blood!. By the age of nine, I had already experienced three traumatic events in my life and, I still remember those traumatic events, as you can see, today. Unfortunately, those traumatic events, would be the first three, of a slew of traumatic events, that would last, throughout the next forty-eight years of my fifty, one years of young life today.

Right after that vacant lot experience, a few months later, me and, my two, older brothers, it was only three of us at this time, we were playing on our three story, wooden back porch, with some of the neighbors kids downstairs, who were known to be bullies and, fowl! Mouth little kids. The oldest girl of the three siblings was around my oldest brother's age, maybe eleven or twelve. She had gone into their apartment and, gotten her parents, pellet gun and, my oldest brother was taunting her, by jumping on the porch landing, side to side. He kept telling her, you can't shoot me! You can't shoot me! I'm too fast for you!.

She began aiming the pellet gun at my brother and, shooting the metal, small pellets at him and, each time that she missed hitting him, the other kids would laugh and, say, you missed! Him! You can't shoot!. But, after a few more misses, she shot! The pellet at my brother one more time, as he tried to leap again, to dodge the pellet. Unfortunately, it struck my brother right on the side of his forehead, just above his eye, as a stream of red blood started to skeet! Out of his forehead!. I began to scream! In terror, traumatized! With all of the other kids screaming too, as my brother grabbed his forehead, crying and, trying to stop the blood that was rushing from, the tiny, pellet hole, in his forehead.

Everyone took off running! Inside of the girls house! As I ran up the stairs, as fast as I could, to go and, tell my mother that my brother had been shot! In the forehead, by the neighbor's daughter, downstairs, with a pellet gun!. Had that pellet hit my brother in the eye, he would have lost his eye permanently, that day. As I said, these kids were known to curse like a sailor and, fight with me and, my two brothers all the time. Their mother I believe was a single parent, of three or four kids around our age, but she had a lot of people always partying and, hanging around her house. My mother had told me and, my brothers to stay away from these kids, many times, because the kids were always fighting with other kids all the time.

Out of our disobedience to what my mother had told us not to do, we went down to their second, floor porch and, this was the end result of us defying our mothers warnings. My oldest brother was shot in the head, with a pellet, by this mean, young girl. My oldest brother got hurt and, had to be rushed to the hospital and, the doctor that saw him removed the pellet from his forehead. My brother received a couple of stitches, to close up the tiny hole in his forehead. What a lesson me and, my two brothers learned that day, for disobeying my mother's warnings about messing with those kids. We were safe, as long as we stayed up on our own porch, where we were protected by my mother and, father's rules. Once we stepped outside of our safety zone that our parents had around us and, we stepped right into the enemy's territory, our safety net was now gone!. Our parents could no longer protect us, from outside of their nest! Their will for us. Do you see the picture, as I paint it out for you and, my points made?.

That's the same thing that happens to us, when we go outside of the will of God and, we try to do things our way. We get involved in the sins of this world, with the wrong type of people and, we get ourselves into all sorts of trouble not knowing that in the end, there is a price to pay. There will be consequences for our poor choices, decisions and, actions that we chose to do. If we do not be careful at some of the choices and, decisions that we make, without confirming it with our Lord first, it can cost us in our relationships with our loved ones, within our marriage, family, your income, your health, even your mental stability and, sometimes you can lose your life!. Sometimes, it can take weeks, months, even years, to repair some of the damage from your past or present bad choices that we make. Unfortunately, some things and, relationships that we damaged, can never be repaired as well. We have to seperate ourselves, from the sins and, cares of this world, for our own good!.

In the scriptures in Ephesians Ch. 5 Vs. 7 Th 11 it reads,

[7] Be not ye therefore partakers with them. [8] For ye were sometimes darkness, but now are ye light in the Lord: walk as children of light: [9] (For the fruit of the Spirit is in all goodness and righteousness and truth;) [10] Proving what is acceptable unto the Lord. [11] And have no fellowship with the unfruitful works of darkness, but rather reprove them. Amen!.

Talk about a young girl not being able to win for losing! From experiencing so many traumatic events and, experiences in my life right? Geezz!. Have you ever felt like, everytime you got yourself out of one bad or stressful situation, you found yourself going back into another situation again?. It's like no matter how hard you try to recover from the last situation, the sudden attacks just start lining up against you. You feel like your enemies are taking turns, hi fiving! Eachother, with your emotions, feelings and, just wearing you out! With stress and, problems.

Sometimes we may even wonder, do you have a sign plastered across your forehead that says, all problems are welcomed to find you!. I know exactly how you feel here. Some days, it gets to the point where you don't want to talk to anyone about what you are going through, you mentally shut down, and, you just want to isolate yourself away from everyone and, be left alone!. In some cases it's okay to get into a quiet place to regather and, regroup your thoughts. It's okay to sit before God, for a while, and seek God's guidance and, strength in those weary moments that many of us have, including myself. We also have to understand, too, that there will be some people who don't want to hear you talk and, vent to them about your problems all the time. It's not that everyone in your life does not care about what you are going through, no. Many people have their own, personal problems that they too, may be going through and, they are dealing with their own, private boughts, just as you. Don't take it personally, when others can't help you, the way that you feel, that they should. Then, you have the other half of the people, who are just glad it's you going through and, not them!. They may be able to help you, but they just won't and, that's life.

You will find out oftentimes in life too, that some people who are suffering, possibly, like you (Us) or who are in a much worse situation, with problems themselves, they are the ones who will sit on the phone with you for hours, to lend an ear, in your time of need. They don't mind you talking about your problems to them, as they talk to you about their problems, in hopes of bringing some comfort to each other somehow. That can be a good and, bad thing, so, be careful, when you are talking to people, about your problems, who may need just as much counseling and, therapy as you!.

I know it, because that used to be me on the phone, talking to people that were just as messed up as I was! Telling them all my problems and, neither one of us could help each other. We were just going through our emotions and, feelings, but did we really solve each other's problems? No we did not. Some of you know what I am talking about, because that probably used to be you too and, maybe still you today. Then you wonder when you get off the phone with them, why you are even more depressed about your situation, than, before you got on the phone with them?. We have to watch those negative and, toxic traits that you can draw from other people, familiar spirits can identify with each other well. If you got one, well balanced, good, stable minded friend or a family member that you can trust, with your situation that you may be facing, stick with that one person. Everyone! Does not need to know all about your problems, especially, if they are not trustworthy or stable in their own lives. Two broken people together, cannot help each other get out of the box. You want to confide in someone, who has solid, stable advice, that can help you along the way. That's just like a person, who has been married and, divorced a few times, but now they want to give somebody advice, about how to stay married. I mean, are you kidding me!? They couldn't even stay married to the first person that they married, and, now three to four marriages later, now, they are an expert! At giving people advice about marriage?. No! Please, stay clear of these people's advice at all cost! For your future marriage. Get around some people, who have withered the storms of life, but their tree bears healthy and, good fruits!. As I said, there are some great counselors and, therapist out here that can also help guide you through what you may be going through and, provide you with coping skills and, teaching skills, to help you along the way towards a better you.

I think about it now, all of that wasted time that I (We) have spent, talking to others about our problems, who never helped me to overcome my situations. I (We) could have been, using that time, talking to medical professionals to help me, and, also, spending time, praying to the Lord, to call out my name! Ask me Where Art Thou!? To comfort and, rescue me, in my times of need. It says, in the scriptures in Psalms Ch. 147 Vs. 3 th 6 it reads here, [3]He healeth the broken in heart, and bindeth up their wounds.[4] He telleth the number of the stars; he calleth them all by their names.[5] Great is our Lord, and of great power: his understanding is infinite.[6] The LORD lifteth up the meek: he casteth the wicked down to the ground. Amen!. God wants to know, where are we at in our lives? Because he cares about our needs and, where we are headed. He wants us to put our full trust in him and, not all in man, woman, boy or girl. Remember as I said earlier, people will fail you, your spouse may even fail you, your family and, friends may fail you, your job! May fail, but, God! Almighty! Never will!. We have to stop treating God, as if he is not God!. God is a God! Who cannot! Lie! And, his word will never! Come back void!. It says, in Isaiah Ch. 55 Vs. 11 it reads, So shall my word be that goeth forth out of my mouth: it shall not return unto me void, but it shall accomplish that which I please, and it shall prosper in the thing whereto I sent it!. Amen!

I pray that I am helping somebody and, setting a lot of you free! From the shackles! Of the enemy in your life. All we have to do, is put your trust in the Lord and, you will never! Be steered wrong, misguided, misused, hurt, lied upon and, be betrayed by the promises and, word of the Lord. It's time to let go! Of the toxic! And, negative! Behaviors of people, these broken family patterns, cycles and, allow Christ to set you free!. Amen! You will have to do the work, as well, to advance your life, to heal and, make healthier choices, that will benefit your growth!. God is not going to do the work, all for you and, just drop your healings out of the sky, no! It's not that simple. God will provide an escape! Door for us and, set us on the right path, yes he will. But, the work as I said earlier, begins within us!. We must begin the work, as we still hold on to our faith, as God sees us through!. It will require time, patience, discipline, commitment and, prayer as well, but, change is possible for us all! if you want it. Amen! Let's continue further here.

I can only imagine how frustrated Jesus was at times, as he was training and, teaching his twelves chosen Apostles, about the ways and, life of his father and, grooming them for the day, that he would be with them physically no more. I can only imagine Jesus sitting with the Apostles and, some of the women who were followers and, teachers as well with the men, how did they behave at times?.

Remember, some of these disciples had to leave behind their wife, children and, families, with nothing but the clothes on their backs and, shoes on their feet, to be followers of the Lord. Now, they are no longer able to share physical intimacy with their wife, they aren't able to go back home and, kiss, touch and, hold their wife, children or family anymore. The disciples of Jesus, they had to give up everything! That they loved and, possessed, to be a true follower, Apostle and, servant of the Lord, for the Kingdom of God!.

They couldn't go back and, hang out with their friends and, roam about the lands, everything in their lives now revolved around Jesus Christ, our Savior and, Lord. Their mission with Jesus was to spread the good news! The gospel of the Lord and, to help lead as many lives to Christ, at their will. They ministered to the lost souls, delivering and, healing the sick, diseased, the blind, the lame, those who were filled, with demonic spirits and, Jesus healed the broken hearted. Can you imagine, if it is a struggle for many of us Christians today, who are serving the Lord, through all the distractions that are around us daily. Can you imagine the stress and, uncertainty that some of the disciples had to have at times too, with Jesus?. They were persecuted and, hated for being a follower of Jesus Christ, teaching and, spreading the gospel of God's word. Most of the time, the ground was their beds, wherever they may have traveled and, whoever's home, that would take them in and, feed them, as they traveled from place to place, by foot and, boat for days at a time. Those places were home to them as they traveled.

Jesus and, his disciples went everywhere to spread the good news of God and, Jesus showed his power, through many of his healings and, deliverance before the people. Can you imagine how exhausted they all probably were at times, from the long walks from town to town, ship rides, enduring the hot sun! And, fighting daily against the people! The Sauducees and, Pharisee's who wanted them all dead!.

Jesus was with the disciples for three years, as they continued to face assaults and, false accusations from the religious leaders and, the people who refused God!. Don't you believe by one thought, that the disciples didn't have some of the struggles that we too suffer with today, as followers of the Lord. As I said, there were women in the midst of the Apostles and, Jesus as well, who also played a big part in spreading the gospel of God, as they traveled from land to land.

The women who followed Christ, also had to leave their families behind, along with all of their possessions, to be a follower of the Lord. Even though the women that followed Christ and, the Apostles don't get enough recognition in the world or within many of the churches today, as they should. Women are frowned upon, shamed! And, even threatened! By many, for wanting to speak and, share the messages of God, especially within, many churches, not all, but, many.

When Jesus died and, he rose on the third day, he showed himself to Mary Magdalene, first, at the tomb where his body was laid. It reads in the scriptures here in John Ch. 20 Vs. 18 Th 22 it reads, [18] Mary Magdalene came and told the disciples that she had seen the LORD, and that he had spoken these things unto her.[19] Then the same day at evening, being the first day of the week, when the doors were shut where the disciples were assembled for fear of the Jews, came Jesus and stood in the midst, and saith unto them, Peace be unto you.[20] And when he had so said, he shewed unto them his hands and his side. Then were the disciples glad, when they saw the LORD.[21] Then said Jesus to them again, Peace be unto you: as my Father hath sent me, even so send I you.[22] And when he had said this, he breathed on them, and saith unto them, Receive ye the Holy Ghost. Amen! There were women and, men present in that room.

God commissioned them all to go teach the word of God across the lands everywhere, heal the sick, free the demonic possessed and, share the gospel of the Lord, for the kingdom of God. There was no division between the men and, women that followed Jesus and, were disciples of Jesus, as it is today. When God spoke to his Apostles and followers, after his resurrection, he told them all to go and, spread the gospel. Jesus did not say, you women who have been my followers, from the beginning, you cannot go! And, witness to the lost, about the living word of God, because you are a woman!. That is not written in the word of God! As Jesus law, against women. Amen!

Let me go into detail here, before some people start throwing rocks! And, boulders! At me.

In the beginning of the Bible God created man and, women in his own image. It says, in Genesis Ch. 1:27; 5:1-2 it reads, in chapter 1

Vs. 27 So God created man in his own image, in the image of God created he him; male and female created he them. Amen! Ch. 5 Vs. 1-2 reads, This is the book of the generations of Adam. In the day that God created man, in the likeness of God made he him; V. 2 Male and female created he them; and blessed them, and called their name Adam, in the day when they were created. Amen!

As we can see here through God's word, God created man and, woman equal! In his own image. Women were prominent in the ministry of the early church, when you find the time read, Acts 12:12-15; 1Cor. 11:11-15. When the New Testament church was born, women were even present there with the chief disciples, praying, read Acts 1:12-14.

Throughout the Bible women have always been praised! For their good works and, deeds of supporting the ministry of God, supporting their husbands and, taking care of their children. But, in today's time, women are not always acknowledged and, honored within many church settings and, Jesus loved and, cared deeply for the women. Like Mary, Martha and, Lazarus whom Jesus raised from the dead, Jesus loved Mary, Martha and, Lazarus. It says, in John Ch. 11 Vs. 5 it reads in a short verse here, Vs. 5 Now Jesus loved Martha, and Mary and, Lazarus. Amen!. Mary was the young woman, when Jesus and, the disciples had come to visit them, anointed Jesus' feet with the oil that she had, with her hair, which was a very expensive oil. You can find this story in John Ch. 12 Vs. 3.

Jesus had a profound love and, respect for women, read about, the Samaritan woman that Jesus spoke to so, kindly and, lovingly at the well. Jews were known, to not have any dealings with the Samarian people, and, especially not speaking in public, to a woman! Who could be stoned! For this. Then there was faithful Anna! Who worshiped the Lord and, she helped to spread the gospel of the Lord throughout Jerusalem, read Luke 2: 36-38 for the story. And, let's not forget about Lydia! Who was also a worshiper and, supporter to the ministry of Jesus read, Acts 16:14 for the story. Amen!

Women were always present throughout the Bible, supporting

Jesus and, his disciples mission, by spreading the gospel of the Lord. The women were not ashamed, because they were women or set apart from the men by Jesus. I can go on and, on, about the women who served a great part of Jesus and, the Apostles Ministry and, spreading the gospel of the Lord!. I hope that I have helped to open up some of your understanding here, about the women whom were followers of the Lord. I pray that, hopefully, many of my readers can have a better respect for some of the women who followed the Lord and, the power! Of influence that these great women had, for the kingdom of God, back then and, even, today!.

The women who were followers of the Lord, were even there with Jesus, as Jesus took his last breath at the cross, talking to his father. Read Matthew Ch. 27: Vs. 55 The 66 Mary Magdalene was present, Mary the mother of James and, Jose and, the mother of Zebedee's children and, Jesus mother were all at the Cross!. Amen!. Read the scriptures and, see for yourself, how important women were, to Jesus, to the ministry of Jesus and, his teachings. Amen!

As a child growing up, I never saw that unconditional love of God, by the men I saw, towards women. I grew up in a family from my father's side, where a couple of my aunties were physically beaten and, mentally abused by the men in their past lives. I had a lot of my female cousins, who were also, as myself too, beaten and, abused by their children's father or boyfriend. As I said, my mother was a victim of domestic abuse, at the hands of my father for twenty years or so. And, a couple of my uncles, had their share of physical abuse, towards their wife and, the women in their lives at that time, too.

I was a child raised within a family that didn't show much love and, respect for each other. And, some of my relatives suffered throughout their life with substance abuse, alcohol abuse and, mental health disorders, within both sides of my parents' family generation. I never saw any affection within my family growing up, other than the love that I received from my father and, my mother's, mother, both my grandmother's, may they rest on now, I pray with the Lord.

I got a lot of my understanding about that unconditional love that we are supposed to have for one another, through the word of God, watching my oldest brother's life as a fifteen, year old young man, who was saved in Christ and, from the church leaders within my childhood church home back, in the 80s when I got saved, with my oldest, brother.

My father had a horrible childhood, he told me and, his father did not raise him, or his other siblings, he was raised in a single parent home in the backwoods of Philadelphia Mississippi. But, my father was one of the smartest! And, most intelligent men that you would ever know when he was sober. He had multiple skills, self-taught, by himself, even though he was illiterate, he could not read, but, my father's wisdom and, skills that he possessed, was far beyond his time!. He was what they called, a Jack! Of all Spades! Hands down! You could not touch his mastery! Of work skills! And, crafts that he knew how to do!.

As I said, my father could do professional, electrical work, plumbing, heating, laying pipes in the ground, he could take a car apart and, rebuild it piece by piece. He was a carpenter, he gutted buildings out and, houses for a living, remodeling them back over again. My father laid cement, built garages, he was a roofer and, a professional fisherman. He and, my grandmother were gardeners too, my grandmother had a garden in the backyard of her home, where my father and, her lived.

I can go on and on talking about the skills that my father self-taught himself, from a child, trying to survive, in the South of the Mississippi's dirt roads. Cancer of the lungs took the strongest and, most brilliant! Man that I had ever known, at only sixty, four years young out from this world.

My father had everything in my eyes but, that unconditional love, he did not know how to love and, treat my mother or any woman with the respect and, love of God. My father was very cruel towards the women he dealt with besides my mother. My father left my mother, for a young lady, who was about twenty five years younger than him,

(In her twenties). And, he fathered a daughter with this young lady, while still being married to my mother, whom he never divorced. Not to mention he had also fathered two sons by another woman, before he met this young girl and, had a daughter. There was a total of three children, that my father, fathered in his marriage with my mother

My poor mother knew about all the other women and, other children that my father had outside of their marriage. But, my mother had no voice with my father, he controlled her, the money he made and, my mother had no family members in Chicago to support her. If my father had not left my mother for the younger woman, my mother would have never left him sad to say. My mother felt like my father was all that she knew from a young girl, she had five children by him, no money and, only a highschool education. She didn't have any friends, so, where else in this big city could she go, with no money, five children, no job or family support?. This is a lot of other women's stories today, who are trapped in abusive relationships and, they feel as if they have no way out. I will talk about that more, later.

Now, my parents did have some good days together when I was a young child. I would sit and, watch my parents sit together in the kitchen at times, as they cleaned and, cooked the fish that my father and, my grandmother caught, when they would go fishing often. He and, my mother would be laughing and, talking as my father seasoned and, cooked the fish in the hot, cast iron skillet that he loved to fry meats in.

I would watch my mother sit on her knees, behind my father's back, as he sat on the edge of the bed when he was home from work. And, she would comb through his short, black, thick afro, scratching the dandruff out of his scalp and, oiling it with the clear, Crown Royal hair grease that she used in his hair and hot, combed pressed my hair with. I could see how relaxing my mother's hands were to my father's head and, how pleased my mother was, doing his hair, as she chewed on a piece of her Day's Work Chewing Tobacco in the side of her jaw. When my father and, mother went grocery shopping together with my grandmother, sometimes in her station wagon, at the famous,

Black folks, One Stop Grocery Store, down by forty third and, Lake Park, here in Chicago.

They would come back with all the groceries and, boxes of meat that they bought for us to eat, putting the food away, side by side. At that time, in the 70s, it was only me and, my two older brothers who were born. I loved to see my parents smiling, laughing together and, preparing our meals together in the kitchen as they talked and, enjoyed each other's company sometimes. Unfortunately, I saw more bad days between them than good days. If I may say, when my father drank alcohol, he turned into a person that you didn't want to be around and, all he knew was physical violence and, rage!.

Those small, little moments of affection that I did see between my parents, was the love I felt my parents had for one another, and, that was the love that I wanted from my own husband one-day, without all of the abuse and, rage!. It was that feeling of togetherness and, small tokens of intimacy without the actual act of sex, that was that unconditional love that I longed to have in my life, with a husband of my own. My mother felt safe and, protected by my father when he was not abusive towards her. She knew he was capable of going to work, keeping the rent and, bills paid for his family, despite what he was doing out in those streets. I wanted that part of my father also, in my husband, one who protected me and our family and, he was reliable to keep the bills paid. Unfortunately, I never found any of that within a mate, a husband in my life.

Most of the friends that I knew coming up, they didn't come from a home, where their parents showed much love for one another either. Within my friends' homes, there was no father present, only the mother and, the homes that did have father's present, the women stayed home to be housewives and, raise the children.

Most of the husband's were always gone, ten to twelve hours a day at work. Most of the men were heavy drinkers, even dabbled in some form of drugs and, they messed around on their wife with other women often. There was physical abuse going on in some of my friends' homes, where the men were cursing and, beating up on the women too. Even though the men paid the rent and, bills for their families, the women still paid a heavy price, for the abuse and, mistreatment that they suffered, at the hands of their husband or the children's fathers. I witnessed this often throughout my childhood, in many of the homes with children and, I could not understand why there was so much abuse and, division between the man, woman and, sometimes even with the children.

I was taught within the church that men were supposed to be the head of the home leading and, guiding their wife and, children in God's word, which was supposed to be good. But, I didn't see a lot of that affection and, love going on in my family or my friends family, where the men were treating the women well and, taking care of their children's needs.

All I grew up watching from a young girl, was abusive patterns and, cycles within my family and, the friends' homes that I knew.

In the scriptures in Ephesians Ch. 5 Vs. 25 Th 33 it reads, Husbands, love your wives, even as Christ also loved the church, and gave himself for it; [26] That he might sanctify and cleanse it with the washing of water by the word, [27] That he might present it to himself a glorious church, not having spot, or wrinkle, or any such thing; but that it should be holy and without blemish. [28] So ought men to love their wives as their own bodies. He that loveth his wife loveth himself. [29] For no man ever yet hated his own flesh; but nourisheth and cherisheth it, even as the Lord the church: [30] For we are members of his body, of his flesh, and of his bones. [31] For this cause shall a man leave his father and mother, and shall be joined unto his wife, and they two shall be one flesh. [32] This is a great mystery: but I speak concerning Christ and the church. [33] Nevertheless let every one of you in particular so love his wife even as himself; and the wife see that she reverence her husband. Amen!

According to these Scriptures, this is the way that God designed men and, women to treat each other in love, towards one another, respecting one another and, supporting one another's needs. The husband in the home is supposed to help establish good values, morals, discipline and, healthy structure within his family with his wife's support. Whatever a child grows up and, experiences or witnesses within their social environment, nine times out of ten, that child will grow up affected by that behavior and, also exemplifying the same patterns of violence, abuse and, negative behaviors that they witnessed, from their parents or peers.

I know, because I became a victim of some of the same physical, emotional and, mental abuse by men in relationships and, within the two marriages that I had to leave. Similar situations that my mother went through with my father, with mental, emotional and, physical abuse. Many women or young girls who have been victims of domestic violence, most of the time, were raised in an environment, where they witnessed some form of abuse within their environment.

Your social environment plays a big role in how you, and, your children respond in life. I know a lot of you, who are reading this book, may have experienced some of the same type of mental, physical and, emotional abuse in your families or within your own relationships as well. These vitous patterns and, cycles of physical, emotional and, mental abuse can traumatize and, affect a child or adult in their life, for many years. Especially, if they do not receive counseling or psychiatric treatment to help them to overcome their trauma.

We ask ourselves at times, how did it happen? Or how did we ourselves get into these destructive patterns of life?. We learn these negative conditions, affects, patterns, cycles and, behaviors from someone who had a powerful influence on us negatively or many others were forced into this lifestyle of abuse or addiction as well. There are thousands of young and, older adults, men and, women who didn't recover from those traumatic experiences of their life.

Stress, fear, peer pressure and, hanging around the wrong type of negative and, toxic people in your life, can play a heavy role, on some of the poor choices and, decisions that we have made in our lives too. As one of my dear friends would say, one false! Move can cost you everything!. God says in his word, that we are to be gentle as Doves, But, wise! As serpents! Because the enemy is always roaming about, to see whom he can devour!. Choose the type of company that you keep around you or in your circle of friends carefully and, seek God at every decision and, choice that you make in your life, first!.

I thank the Lord, because God loved me so much and God gave me many chances to get my life right! With him. I pray that you are being blessed here so far as I continue on, further.

Have you ever been in a place in your life, where you start thinking back, to all of the wrong choices and, decisions that you have made, that put yourself and, family in harm's way?. Just dumb! Choices when you think about it today and, you say to yourself why did I do that?. Why did I even choose to deal with him or her anyway? Or why did I marry him or her?. You wonder now that you can see your mistakes, what on God's earth! Was I thinking when I did this and, that?. I see some of you can relate here to what I am saying, I know right?.

A lot of the poor choices and, decisions that we made in life, may have caused some of you (Us) a ripple effect of losses, because we didn't confirm it with God first. Instead we tried to do it our way, or others way and, in the end we crashed! And, burned!. Sometimes it's not others that lead us astray, sometimes it's you (Us) we lead ourselves astray and, the only person at times that we can point the finger at, in some situations is ourselves. There are times in our lives, if we don't be careful and, seek God's direction first, you yourself (I) can be your own worst! Enemy, you!.

The scriptures says, here in Matthew Ch. 6:33 it reads,

[33] But seek ye first the kingdom of God, and his righteousness; and all these things shall be added unto you. Amen! There is absolutely nothing wrong with going to people that you trust for advice, but when it comes down to life changing situations, I would suggest to you, to please take it to the Lord in prayer and, wait for God to give you confirmation about your situation first. Even if a friend, family or spiritual leader gives you some advice about something, make sure that what they are telling you, aligns with the word of God.

Ask God to give you a spirit of discernment, to be able to see what type of spirits you are connecting yourself with. As I said before, wolves can camouflage and, make you think that they are a pretty teddy bear or innocent kitten before you. In these wicked times that we are living in, you better do a complete background! Check! On anyone that you allow into your personal space, especially around your children and, family.

Some people come with motives and, hidden agendas as to why they want to be around or attach themselves to you. There are a lot of users, lier's, manipulator's and, narcissistic men and women out here, looking for prey, a victim like you (Us) to gaslighting and harm. To the men, that woman can be sitting right across from you at the table, she's looking gorgeous and, innocent just like Mary Popkins! And, at the same time, she may be the wicked! Witch! Of the West! Hidden in disguise!. To the women, he can act and, look just like Denzel Washington, put on a great presentation before you and, act like the Catholic Pope! Sitting there. But, underneath all of those good looks, he can be a Freddy! Kruger! In disguise!.

HELLO! My readers, I'm trying to help save a lot of you here, from hooking up with the wrong people, just because they may look good on the outside and, they may be dark! As charcoal! In their heart! On the inside. You have to pay attention to all! The red flags and, signs that God gives you about the people you surround yourself with today. The older folks used to say, that everything that looks like glitter! Is not Gold!. The enemy has his way of putting things in front of you, that he knows you like or have a weakness for, he knows you better than you think. He will dress it up, let it look good, smell so good! Speak politely and, all. But underneath all of those fancy suits, fancy dresses, pants, make-up and, hair it's a time! Bomb! Waiting to happen and, explode!. It's a walking garbage! Truck! That is rotten! And, stinks! Underneath all of that pretty and, handsome smiles.

You gotta see people with four eyes and, God's eyes I say today. I pray that you are protecting your sanity, your heart, and your spirit, through reading and, studying the word of God in prayer, at all times!.

Everyday we must keep on our armor! For your protection as the Bible says, we should be doing. Amen! Okay you got this!.

If I knew back then growing up, what I know today, now, I would be in a much better place in my life at fifty, one years young today. There are a lot of things that I have done, that I would not have ever done and, a lot of people that I allowed into my life, that I would have never! Given a thought to. But, I have learned so much, from my past mistakes, that have made me a better person in my life today..

My parents were raised, with poor parenting skills from their parents and, peers so, they couldn't pour into me, and my siblings what they themselves did not have. I realize now that my parents did the best that they could with us five kids, with the skills and, love that they had to give us. It was because of the love that my parents gave to me, that helped me to become a better woman and, mother to my own, three children and, my grandchildren as well.

As I got older, I better understood the life that my parents were raised in, than the life that many of us take, for granted at times. I stopped blaming them for the mistakes that I made in life and, I became appreciative for the love and, care that my parents did give to us, in their own ways. My father didn't leave my mother or us until we were young adults, with children of our own. So, hey, we had a father around through those toughest teenage years, when children needed their father present in the home, with the mother. Me and, my sister took over, taking care of the needs of our mother dear, making sure that her life was now at peace and, her needs were met.

Even though I made a lot of poor decisions and, choices in my life, I am who I am, because of the struggles that I saw my parents go through. My father's strong! Arm! Of disciplining us with his belt! Kept us out of the prison system at least four of us out of the five of us and, out of the five of us, three of us have college education and, one of my siblings went to trade school. I have no hatred or unforgiveness in my heart towards my parents. I love my mother who is well today and, my father when he was alive, because of the life that they tried hard to provide for their children, with the little that they had.

The scriptures says here in, Ephesians Ch. 6 Vs.1 Th 3 it reads, **6** Children, obey your parents in the Lord: for this is right.² Honour thy father and mother; which is the first commandment with promise;³ That it may be well with thee, and thou mayest live long on the earth. Amen!

No matter what we may feel or think about our parents, whether it be good or bad, God says that we are to honor our parents period!. I know that there may be a lot of my readers who may have been sexually abused, physically and emotionally abused by a parent or both parents. There are many people who have suffered at the hands of their parents and, have not healed from that trauma or found it in their heart to forgive them.

I am not here to judge or condemn you or anyone for what you may have suffered at the hands of an abuser. I have never been abused by a parent in that manner, therefore I cannot relate to your pain. But, I can say this, despite the abuse that I witnessed from my father beating my poor, innocent mother for many years and, from the five, men that sexually raped and, harmed me in my youth, I had to give all of that pain over to God and, forgive them all, in order for me to heal. The burdens were too heavy for me to continue carrying.

I carried that pain and, unforgiveness in my heart and, spirit for about thirty five years of my life and, it was killing my light inside of me and, the blessings that God had for me. Holding on to all of the resentment and, anger was even affecting my mental stability and, health. Harboring around, all of that unforgiveness did not make me a better person, it made me bitter and, just hating the world, for what had been done to me. Once I was able to ask God to take all of that rage, anger, fear, sadness, hurt, pain, distrust and, unforgiveness out of my heart and I was healed. I felt better about myself as, I got the mental and, emotional help that I needed and, I learned how to love and, trust people again.

The best part about my healing was, I got to lead my father, days before he passed away to God!. Wheewh! I'm about to start crying here. Had I held on to that anger, against my father, God would not have been able to use me, to help welcome my father into the kingdom of heaven!. My father would have died unrepentant of his sins and, lost his soul to Hell!. Because of the love that I had for my father and, me fully forgiving him, for all the things he had done to my mother, I will see my father I believe, in heaven again!. Amen!. Releasing unforgiveness in your heart, against your victimizers and, abusers that healing and, growth is for you! (Us). Amen!.

I pray for those of you that are reading my book, if you are still holding on to hurt, pain and, unforgiveness in your heart against anyone that has harmed you, hurt you and, betrayed your trust in them. I pray that you take that pain, before the throne of God, in your alone time. Ask God to help you free! Yourself! From those bondages! Yokes! And, strongholds! That the enemy is holding you hostage to so, that you can heal and, release that pain over to God!. Watch how God lifts those burdens off of your life and, God will move you forward, to start another fresh chapter of your life with God, guiding you through! Amen!

CHAPTER 3

Love Don't Love Nobody?- But God's Love Is True.

AT FIFTEEN YEARS young I had my first, born son as a Southmore in High School. I attended the old Englewood High School back in the 80s, on the Southside of Chicago. It was one of the many school's, that Rahm Emanuel, our former mayor, ordered to be converted or closed down, with hundreds of other schools, in our poor communities, before leaving office in 2019. After having my son, my highschool days were now over, because I now had a son to take care of. I wined up like most improvised, Black mothers with children, on what they called AFDC, welfare at that time.

My little, adorable son brought me so much joy, looking down at his sweet, innocent little face, when I held him in my arms. I used to sing this song by this artist, by the name of "Mint Condition" and, the song was called "Pretty Brown Eyes". My baby boy had the prettiest, dark brown eyes, when I looked into his eyes, as I held him in my arms. And, all I could think of was that song, when I smiled and, kissed his beautiful cheeks. My oldest brother was crazy about my baby, when he was born. My brother would pray over my baby for me, when he would be sick often, suffering from asthma.

Even though I was young and, vulnerable my baby, my son was my everything and, the reason for me to live! And, take care of him. My father was upset of course when he found out that I was pregnant, and, my mother never said too much about it at all. As I said, my mother never really had a voice in the house, so, to her there was nothing that could be done about it anyway. But, once my son was born and, he began to walk, he brought so much joy! To my mother and, father with his smiling little face. He was a happy, cute little boy, always hugged up with me or my mother and he wasn't a baby that cried alot, but, he stayed sick all the time.

I came home from my friend's house one day and, there was my father, sitting in his chair, in front of our small, black and, white television, that was sitting on top of a broken! Floor model television that we had. I know some of you had that same set up in your family's house, with the small television, sitting on top of the wooden, floor model television, right?. My father had my little, one year old baby boy, sitting on one of his thighs, feeding him some of his food that he was eating. That was one of the most special and, precious moments for me to see my father with his grandson, showing him his love and, care for him.

My mother would watch him sometimes and, let me hang out with my friends and, when I got my first job at Taco Bell Downtown, my mother would watch my baby so that I could go to work. I did realize that I needed to get a job, to better take care of the needs of me and, my son because being on Public Aid was not enough. My son stayed sick a lot as a little one year young toddler and, it was detected by the doctors that he had a high level of lead poisoning in his blood, from the paint chips on the walls. Back then in the 80's the paint on the walls in many, old buildings, were full of dangerous lead and, many children at that time, were being affected with lead, in their bloodline. The lead from the paint made a lot of children sick, and, even mentally challenged, with severe health issues, that could last through their adulthood years.

There were a lot of landlords being fined by the state and, sued in court by families of children who got lead poisoning from the paint on the walls. There was a Board Of Health Clinic, about twenty blocks away from our building that we lived in and, I had to walk every week, with my son there, to get his blood and, urine constantly tested.

The nurses had to give my son these shots, every week, that were supposed to reduce the lead levels in his blood. And, I had to put this urine bag over his private area, to catch some of his urine once a week, then walk his urine back to the clinic, to get checked, to see if the lead levels were dropping from the shots that the nurses were giving my son, weekly. We didn't have money to ride the buses at that time and, I wasn't working then, so, every week, I had to walk with my son in my arms, twenty, long, blocks to the clinic and, back home. It took about two, years of these medical treatment shots, before the levels of lead finally went down at a normal range, in my baby's blood. I was the happiest young, sixteen year young girl in the world then, because my baby boy was going to be alright and, I know longer had to walk those long blocks with my baby in my arms anymore, winter, spring, summer and, fall. Talk about a hard life that I had, from my mother's womb, it was a struggle!. But, I thank the Lord that my parents, my little sister who was about twelve, at that time, helped me with my son and, my oldest brother supported me as a teenage mother and, didn't turn their backs on me.

There are a lot of young girls, who got pregnant at a young age, still in grammar school or highschool and, their parents threw them out of the house and, the family turned their backs on them. Some of you may not have had the support that I had with my first child, when you got pregnant at an early age and, many of you may have had to suffer, living from place to place or even having to live in a shelter, because you had no place to go. I know that feeling and, experience too, because later in my life, I had to live in a few shelters with my children too. I understand how mentally, emotionally and, physically draining that may have been for some of you. Not to forget to mention, my son's father was not involved in his life, he did not claim his child when he was born. I was a teenager and, my sons father was close to thirty, maybe even thirty years old at that time. He was one of the neighborhood gang leaders and, drug dealers back then. It was best for me, to not even mention to anyone, who my son's father was, for safety reasons, at that time. But, I depended on my family and, God to see me through. Only my prayers and, faith in God almighty got me through those hard, and, terrible times, three children later.

My prayers are for parents who are facing serious issues with a child or children and, I encourage you, to please do not throw your child, or teenager out into the streets, for the wolves! To swallow them up! Out there. There are wolves! Out there waiting and, looking for young, lost, vulnerable youth. You have these predators who sex, traffic young people and, prostitute them for money. These predators put these young people on drugs, pills and, alcohol to control them mentally, emotionally, and, physically. They control them by many ways of force and, enslavement against their will!. Many of these young people never make it out of that lifestyle, once they are forced in and, some of these young people wind up being murdered out there or overdosing on drugs.

You do not want to find out that your daughter or son got pulled into this lifestyle, because you put them out on the streets. And, Lord forbid, you get that phone call, that your daughter or son was found dead while out there in those streets. That is something that you will have to live with, for the rest of your life, in your heart. Many of these young people, who are out there in these streets wind up with diseases and go to jail or prison, coming out with felonies that cannot be expunged as well. Do whatever you have to do with your child, to seek therapy, counseling, rehabilitation services, inpatient, outpatient services and, mental health services. There are many services in your state, to get the help that you need for your son or daughter, if needed, for behavioral and, addiction issues. Don't abandon your son or daughter in their time of need, sit down with them and, find out where the problems are within them, how it began?. Find out what are the issues or trauma that they may be facing. Bring other family members into the conversation if needed, the ones that you can trust, to help you support your son or daughter, even perishoners of the church, if that will help. Sometimes it really does take a village to help raise the children. But, confide in knowledgeable people and, medical professionals that you can trust, always do your research as well first!.

Many of our youth today already feel like they don't have a voice or place in this world. Many of our youth are going through peer pressure, gender identity, depression and, anxiety. Many of our youth are being targeted and, bullied at school and, by cyber bullying as well. Some of our youth, may even be suffering from physical abuse or sexual abuse by family members, parents (A parent) or peer. A lot of our young people hide these abuses out of shame and, fear that no one will believe them. If you are a parent, who's son or daughter are experiencing some type of anger, isolation, depression or anything that may seem out of the unordinary with them, sit down and, find out what is going on with them. Our children have a voice too and, they need to be heard, not silenced!.

My parents didn't say much about me getting pregnant so young, because they felt I had already had the baby and, the damage was already done in their eyes. The friends that I had at that time, one of my friends had a small baby before I did too and, two, of the three of my friends were two and, three years older than me. All three of my closest friends were sexually active, drinking sometimes and, smoking marijuana.

None of my friends had a father in the home, and all three of my closest friends, two girls and, one (Queer) male friend, all three of their mothers had alcohol and, drug addictions. We all were so close to each other, because we could relate to some of the problems with our parents and, peers around us, at home. We were four, lost young people searching in all the wrong places for someone to accept us and, for love.

There was an old saying, that "Birds of a feather, flocked together" and, you are the type of company that you keep. Powerful sayings right?. We tend to cling to the type of people, who are just as broken as we ourselves are in some ways, who we feel understand our struggles. Everyone that I grew up around or that I knew were either living in a home where physical abuse was going on, domestic violence, or had a parent dealing with substance abuse and, alcohol addiction.

There was no father figure in the house and, the presence of God's love, affection, morals and, values of life, was not present within any of our homes. Many of the parents that I knew, just as my own parents, did not take the time to invest in their children's future.

It's very unfortunate today that the cell phones, tablet's, computers and, video games have consumed many of our young people and, adults minds. Those electronic devices have replaced a lot of that precious family time and, bonding time that we should be spending with our family's. The verbal and, physical communication that parents and, spouse should have within their family structure, is not present enough, as it should be, in a lot of homes. You will see within the church services 90% of women in service with their children and,10% of men there with their wife and, children present. The women are there in service, praying for their husband, children, families and, many of the husbands, are working or at home watching the Sunday sports, drinking on a can of beer and, smoking cigarettes etc. And, people wonder why their marriage is in turmoil and, you both are arguing over simple stuff day and, night with your spouse?. The husband's position in the home is for him to lead his wife and, children according to the word of God and, to be a role model for his family. As a young girl, I was always searching for that feeling of love and, safety within the family, like I felt God's presence within our church home, when I attended church, as a child.

I never felt truly loved or experienced it anywhere that I went, but at church, where I felt my safest. I loved to go to church with my oldest brother, right by his side, because I always felt like I was in the presence of God when I was there. I got baptized at twelve years young, I received the holy spirit of God and, I felt like my sins were all washed away, before I had a child. I thought I had a new peace within me then. Unfortunately.....

As I said, by the time I was fifteen years young, I had been sexually assaulted four, separate times against my will, by five different men.

The first assault happened to me, by this teenage boy, while hanging out with my closest cousin, whom we called one another sisters, who was my age. She had taken me with her, to go and, see this young boy that she was dating. When the boy let us in his house, my cousin and, the boy left me in another room, with this other teenager boy. In the room, while I was waiting on my cousin to return, this boy, who was much older than me, forced himself on me and, he raped me. I told my cousin what he had done to me, when we left and, she really didn't say much about it, just that it, was nothing that we could do about it and, her attitude was like, oh well. So, I never spoke about it again to anyone after that, I believed just like she did, that knowone would believe me anyway. I thought to myself, that I should not have gone to that house with my cousin in the first place and, my cousin made me feel like it was my own fault that it happened. I had accepted what happened to me and, I never spoke about it again. I thanked the Lord that I did not get pregnant from the assault, because I was only fourteen years old, with no parenting knowledge at all and, I was a virgin at the time of the assault. I remembered going home, washing up and, talking to God about what just happened to me and, praying for his forgiveness, because I believed it was my fault.

I was assaulted again, a "Second" time, going with my cousin, once again, to get some shoes she said she had left, at her boyfriend's house. I didn't even know that her boyfriend was a grown man, in his twenties at that time and, her boyfriend and, the other guy there was his uncle. My son was born when this incident happened to me and, my mother was watching him for me, but she had no ideal that I was with my cousin this day.

The guy let us into this dusty, marijuana smelling apartment and, I met her boyfriend and, his uncle who looked like he was in his forties. They both were gang members and, had a bad reputation for selling drugs in the area. As soon as I entered that apartment, my spirit told me, something bad was about to happen being in that dark, demonic looking dungeon. My cousin went into a bedroom with her boyfriend, leaving me out there with his creepy, looking uncle. The next thing that I remembered, this guy forced me into another bedroom with him and, sexually assaulted me. I remembered asking him crying and, afraid for our lives, why was he doing this to me and, his response to me was, that he does whatever his nephew tells him to do.

He was blaming his nephew, who was in the other room with my cousin, doing God knows what, for his reasoning for sexually assaulting me against my will. Unbelievable right? They refused to let me and, my cousin leave that apartment, until the next day. I had actually escaped out the front door, when the uncle left the room. I ran down the stairs, out the front door, running up the block, not knowing that my cousin's boyfriend was racing behind me. He caught me by my arm and, made me walk back to the apartment with him, laughing about the fact that I had almost gotten away. They held us against our will, until finally, letting us leave the next day. All I thought about that night, laying on their front coach, was if my baby and, my parents would ever see me again. When me and, my cousin, left that horrible place, I was so angry at her. She apologized to me over and, over telling me that she was sorry, for taking me over there with her and, for what his uncle had done to me. I didn't even think about what might have happened to her. She was my best cousin, someone that I loved and, cared about as my sister. We did everything together as kids and, she was an abused child, by the hands of her mother as well. I did not tell anyone what had happened to me, with my cousin, for a second time. I never went anywhere else with her again and, I don't believe my cousin came back around for a long time after that incident.

You would have thought, after the first incident with her, that I would have never followed behind her ever again right?. She was the only cousin my age, who I had been close with since we were like seven years old and she was like the older sister that I had never had and, always wanted.

We did everything together, when she came over to stay some weekends with me often. Everytime she came around I just loved to be around her, even though she was going through a lot of turmoil from her mother and, fourteen siblings at home. Yes! There were fifteen of them, with three sets of twins between the fifteen or sixteen kids. My cousin was the oldest of the kids, her life was spent rocking, cleaning and, caring for her siblings as a young nine or ten year old child herself. We both were troubled young girls and, in many ways, we gave each other so, much unconditional love and, support when we were together. I had empathy and, love for my cousin, and, she still is my sister to my heart, today. I forgave her for both assaults that happened to me, under her watch.

Me and, my cousin, when we became adults, with our own children, we never talked about the assault, but maybe a couple of times. As I said, she apologized to me and, told me that she was sorry for what happened to me back then. I accepted her apology and, just left the situation at God's throne and, moved on.

My third, sexual assault that happened to me, was by my sons, father's, two, adult twin cousins. I had come over to his house, where he lived with his mother, in this two, flat house, this day looking for him. One of his twin cousins had let me in the house and, he told me that my son's father was upstairs. I knew his older two, twin cousins, from visiting my son's father, so, I trusted his word. As he led me up to the attic apartment, I turned to look behind me and, he had called his brother upstairs behind us.

He then locked the door, as his twin brother came up and, I asked them both what was going on and, where was my son's father?. I began to go into shock, remembering, this is how it happened with my cousin the two, time's that I was sexually assaulted following her. Both of them refused to let me out the door. They were in their late twenties and, much bigger than I was in height. I was fifteen years young and, weighed about a hundred and, twenty pounds at that time. They both threatened me and, told me that I could not leave the attic, unless I did what they said. They both sexually assaulted me and, told me to never tell anyone what occurred that day.

I never told my son's father what his twin cousins did to me that day, because they were all extremely close and, they hung out on the block together, where I hung out with my three friends all the time. My closest, older friend, lived with her mother, grandmother and, sister just five houses away, from my son's father's house, on the same side of the street. I knew that he would not believe me, over his blood cousins. They were grown, well known men in the neighborhood and, I was a nobody, fast! Teenager, hanging around the wrong type of people, you can say. I never even told my family or my friends about any of the sexual assaults that had happened to me, and, for years, no one knew the suffering that was going on inside of me but, God.

I felt like it was my fault, for being in places that I never should have been and, that was my payback, for walking away from the Lord, after my first, sexual assault at fourteen. After that first assault had happened to me, with my cousin, I had stopped going to church and, my brother had signed himself into the Military. When he left for the Military after he graduated from highschool, most of my hopes and, dreams kind of died when he left, because I felt like my oldest brother was my protector. My second, oldest brother never, really lived with us. By the age of twelve, years young, he was living with his childhood friend and, his parents, whom my father knew. My brother wanted to move, with his friend, at the age of twelve, who lived around the corner, alley of our house. My father was close to my brother's friend's father so, he trusted my brother to go and, live with them. After the assaults had happened to me, I felt like my body was contaminated, from all the sexual assaults that had happened to me. I believed that I had lost my spirit of walking faithfully in the Lord and, I was not worthy of anyone's love.

Have you ever been put in a bad situation by someone else, and, you knew in your heart, that you should not have been with them in the first place or you had no business going where you went?. Yes, I know it's a ugly feeling that you have, once the situation is over, you kick yourself almost, thinking how stupid! You were for being there or around that person.

Most victim's of sexual assault, normally blame themselves for what happened to them and, they never tell anyone about the assaults that happened to them, or not until many, years later, as I did. They feel like no one will believe them or support them and, even out of fear, many victims suffer in silence. Many victims of sexual assaults turn to drugs, pills, alcohol and, even promiscuous behavior too, trying to suppress the trauma that they silently live with.

You will be surprised at how many women, men, boys and, girls hide their sexual assault or physical abuse, done to them in today's time, right now from parents, family and, friends. We have to do more, to help protect and, educate our youth and, older adults concerning domestic abuse and, sexual assault. We have to do more, to reach out to victims of any kind of abuse, that their (Our) voices need to be heard and, that they do matter in this world!.

My final sexual assault happened to me, at the hands of one of my father's sisters, son father. My auntie and, her boyfriend lived in the attic of my grandmother's house, with her three sons. She had an older guy, close to forty, I'm not exactly sure of his age, but he was over thirty five and, she had a baby with him, around the same age that my first son was.

Her son's father kidnapped me off the streets one-day, as I was walking home one summer day from a friend's house, several blocks away from my house. He saw me walking, as he was sitting in the back seat of the car, with a guy that was driving the car. He had the guy park the car and, he jumped out the back, passenger door and, started yelling out my name. When I looked over at the car, I saw that it was my auntie's boyfriend and, he called me to come over to the parked car. When I came over to the car, wondering what he wanted, he told me that his friend would drive me home and, that I shouldn't be walking alone, so far from my house.

My house was about eight more blocks away and, I didn't mind walking home. That was how me and, my friends got around when we were teenagers back then, we walked or rode the CTA bus. We didn't have Uber or Lyft at that time, back in the eighties and early 90s. You rode a bike, or called a livery car that was like a cab company, you took the buses or trains and, you walked. I did not want to get into the backseat of the car with my auntie boyfriend, because he was known in my neighborhood, where I lived, for doing drugs with my other best friend, her oldest brother, who was on PCP and, Heroin at that time. They both were doing drugs at my friend's house, together with the women that they were messing around with. When I would go and, hang out with my friend at her house sometimes, my aunt's boyfriend would be there at times, getting high with her brother and, some of his friends.

My auntie used to drive her car over to our house all the time looking for him and, she would have me get in the car with her and, show her where he was hanging out at my friend's house. She somehow knew that her son's father was hanging out near our neighborhood, cheating on her and, doing drugs. I showed her my friend's house, up the street from my house one-day, as I ducked down, hiding in the backseat of her car, as we drove past my friend's house.

My auntie's boyfriend was this big, tall, muscular built guy, who wore a pulled back ponytail in his hair back then. And, I only weighed, as I said earlier, about a hundred and, twenty or thirty pounds at the time and, I stood about five feet five or six. He forced me to allow them to take me home, by grabbing me by my hands and not letting me go.

When he opened the passenger door and, got into the back seat with me, I never made it home to my son, my baby boy, my first, born love who was waiting for me to come home and, kiss his beautiful face. He instructed this guy to drive us to this motel. I will never forget that motel between the 90th and 91st block of Ashland on the Southside of Chicago. It is still there today with a big, white sign that says, Motel, not too far from where my grandmother's house was, where my auntie, her three sons and, him lived. I have passed that motel a dozen times, since that assault happened to me there, by him and, the motel is only about 10 minutes away from my grandmother's house. Every time I pass that Motel, which is not often today, I think about how my auntie's, sons, father assaulted me there, on that day, against my will

My thoughts about this is, he had to have been taking other women to this particular motel, because why would he drive me from one part of the lower end of the South Side of the city, all the way to the upper South West part of the city, right by my grandmother's house?. That was about a thirty minute ride, from where he took me away from my community, against my will, where I lived.

I begged the driver, who looked like he was in his fifties, to please let me out of the car or take me home!. He ignored my pleas, of him not taking me, with my aunties child's father to that motel that day. He just shook his head no, saying that he had nothing to do with it, but he did. I was a young, fifteen year, young teenager, who had been forced into the back seat of his car, against my will. He was also responsible for the assault that happened to me, because he took me with this grown man to a motel, knowing what he was going there to do with a young girl, my age. My auntie's boyfriend kept me at that motel with him until noon, the next day. He sexually assaulted me, during those hours from that late evening, until noon the next day and, I was totally powerless against him and, terrified! For my life. When it was time to go, he told me not to tell anybody about what he had done to me or he would lie about it, because no one would believe me. I remembered him putting thirty dollars in my hand, as I quickly went out the door, walking slowly up the street in shock and, worried about my son, who hadn't seen me since yesterday nor my parents. I never told a soul of this day. I was fifteen years, young and, now, I had been sexually assaulted five times, from the age of fourteen to just fifteen. All within one year, by four adult men and, a teenager young boy. The only thing that kept me mentally sane and, from not harming myself, from my trauma of these assaults, that had been done to me, was my personal relationship that I had with God. Talking to God daily, about my pain and, my first born son, who needed his mother's love and, I needed his love too, that is what kept me alive and, not looking back!.

Later down the years, I believe my auntie's boyfriend and, her had a really bad fight back then, that led to her putting him out and, he told my auntie, to hurt her, that he had slept with her niece, me!. How sick! Of a person this monster was! And, a pedophile rapist! Who had kidnapped me against my will!. He was able to convince my own auntie that I willingly slept with him, as if I was his girl somehow. Instead of my auntie coming to me, now in my twenties or thirties when it got back to me by other family members, she destroyed my name, to other family members, without knowledge of the sexual assault done to me, by her boyfriend. She never, once, asked me what had happened back then between him and I. Instead, my auntie destroyed my reputation, throughout all of my father's relative's and, everyone that she knew, telling them that I slept with her son's father. I was hurt and, I couldn't believe that she would do this to me, her niece. I was the same young girl, her niece, that she would come and, get to ride up and, down the blocks by our house, as she searched for him to come home.

To this day, many of my father's relatives still believe this vicious! Lie! That was told about me by this monster! And, my auntie. My auntie has never come to me about the situation to this day, to talk to me, about what really happened to me thirty, five years ago to me, at the hands of my auntie's sons father. Thank God I had Christ in my life and, I was able to forgive all of these people, five in all, who had sexually assaulted me as a fourteen and, fifteen year old girl. I also, forgive my auntie and, my father's relatives, for their years of slandering my name and, the lies that have been told about me, by them as well. God knows the truth and, my name is cleared! By God!.

This is the reason why a lot of sexually assaulted victims never tell on their victimizers, in fear that they won't be believed and, they will be judged that it was their fault. It doesn't matter to me today, because God was there, when all of the victimizers, all five of them, sexually assaulted me back then. God will have the last say so, on judgment day, when they will stand before God. God says, Vengeance! Shall be mine! Amen!.

I am at peace with it all today and, healed. I don't believe my aunt's son's father is alive today, he was on heavy drugs back then in the early 80s and, 90s. I don't know if he overdosed or died from something else.

When I first got married, I was so glad to get rid of my father's family's last name, Brown, because I had never been treated like a niece by many of his siblings or shown any form of love from them at all. I had a relationship with three of my father's brothers, two are deceased now and, one is still alive, who has two daughters. But, I don't have any relationship with my uncle's two daughters. I was only shown love, by these three uncles throughout my life, out of my father's eleven or twelve siblings, sad to say.

My parents have (Had) no idea about these assaults, because I never got the courage to tell them, or other family members, because of the type of family that I came from, that lacked any family love towards each other. I didn't even trust and, tell my closest friends about everything, but if I had, I know my closest friends would have believed me and, supported me. I didn't want to put my problems on my three friends, because all of their mother's, were hooked on drugs. They were going through their own personal struggles at that time and, I dared not bother them about the things that I had suffered. I just silently dealt with my deep trauma and, depression with the Lord.

For much of my teenage years and, my adult life, I have suffered with depression, anxiety, PTSD, and panic attacks that were undiagnosed for half my life.

Throughout my life, I wondered why these vitous attacks had happened to me? When I had already suffered so, much, after I was born from my mother's womb. After all, I had faith in the Lord since the age of nine, I talked to the Lord, I feared God and, I wanted to serve God. So, why did all of these things I asked myself, happen so traumatically to me?. I guess that is a question, that God will answer for me, in heaven with him one-day. We can ask God, questions concerning our situations, yes we can, but don't expect God to give you an answer, because he doesn't have to. God is God, he is the ruler over every person, nation, government, all demons! And, Satan!. God answers to no one! Just remember that and, when we do get a response back from God, be honored and, thank him! For directing our paths. Job, who suffered greatly in the Bible, didn't get an answer from God, as to why he had to suffer all that he lost, as a justman of God and, innocent before God. He lost all of his cattle, thousands of cattle burned! From fire! Falling from the sky, he lost all of his wealth and, workers too. Job lost all ten of his children and, his grandchildren who were killed! At one setting, eating dinner together, as a wind storm, sent by Satan, caused the house to fall down and, kill all of them!. Job's health was affected, he was hit with some form of disease, all over his body. Job had these huge boils and, blisters from the top of his head, to the bottom of his feets that was extremely! Painful!. And, his body ached all over, his limbs were swollen and, disfigured too. Job could barely breathe on some days, the scripture also says, and, Job had lost all of his healthy weight, the scripture says, that Job was skin! And, bones!. Even Jobs wife turned against him, out of her grief from seeing her husband suffer, losing their children, grandchildren, daughter and son in laws, plus everything that they owned. They were being falsely accused of some type of sin that Job's three friends, Eliphaz, Bildad and, Zophar had claimed, that Job must have committed sin against God. Job's three friends told Job that God was punishing him for his unconfessed sins. Job's wife now sees Job, with these sores all over his body, suffering to the point of death!. Out of her love for her husband, she tells Job to just curse! God! And, Die!. She could not stand to see her husband suffering any longer and, she wanted Job to die, to be put out of his suffering and, misery by God. When you get a chance read starting at Job Ch. 1-2 for the story and, further through the chapters. Job suffered more than anyone in the Bible, as a justman, an innocent man before God the scripture says. God called Job a just man And, that there was none! Like him anywhere, that's a pretty high praise from God about Jobs' character. Furthermore, God never gave Job an answer as to why? He was sifted as wheat by Satan, why he lost everything, his family, possessions and, all that he suffered and, was falsely accused of. In Ch. 42 of Job, God restored Job back more! Than he had lost!. Job and, his wife Sarah had ten more children, Job regained thousands of more cattle and, God made Job's three friends repent before Job, for falsely accusing him of sinning before God. All of the people came and, apologized to Job, with gifts and, Job's reputation was restored in the land, amongst the people. And, we think we have it bad sometimes, not like how Job and, his wife had suffered much loss here. Our situations that we may face in life may be rough, and, make us feel like we have no hope and, our pain will never end, but it will. If we continue to put our faith in the Lord, as Job did, God will give us the strength to overcome our situations at hand. Job never! Cursed God as Satan wanted Job to do, but instead Job continued to proclaim his innocence before everyone and, God. Job believed that God would vindicate his innocence and, Job never lost his faith in God, even in his anger and, great suffering, Job continued to cry out to God in his daily prayers to see him through. Amen!

In the midst of my pains, I had to act normal around my parents, my siblings and, friends as if nothing had ever happened to me, after each sexual assault, that happened to me. My depression was so dark and, I had absolutely no one to confide in, about what I had experienced or what I was going through. I was a young girl, who's life felt like death and, that this world had nothing to offer me. The only hope that I had was praying as a young girl to Christ and, holding my first, born son in my arms, as he held on to me at night. God and, my baby son were my only reasons that I had to live!.

Surprisingly, I never was an angry, young girl despite all the things that had happened to me. Something deep within me, would not allow me to hold on to that poison, in my heart with vengeance. I guess that was the spirit of God that dwelled within me, keeping my heart pure. But as I got older, I continued to be involved in abusive relationships, my depression and, dark days just grew more and, more. It began to take over my emotions, with daily racing thoughts.

I would have panic attacks, several times a week for years, and, insomnia was taking the place of my sleep during many of the nights. I would function as I was supposed to at work, at church, at family functions and, around friends, but that was only the fake mask that

I wore, to hide my silent pain. I did not go and, get the mental help that I needed, until ten years ago. I knew after I was spiraling out of control for so long, on my own, that it was time to go and, get help that I badly needed. It was the best decision that I could have ever made for myself. Now I understand the mental disorders that I have, that have crippled me most of my life. The treatments from seeing my doctors and, psychiatrist have done wonders to help me deal with my trauma and, depression today.

I recently confessed the sexual assaults that had happened to me, to my two, oldest brothers in a long text message, about three years ago. I didn't get the opportunity to express it in a verbal conversation, like I wanted to with them both, because our relationship as siblings is strained and, far off. I have one brother, our youngest sibling, who is incarcerated today. My oldest two, brothers and, my only, younger sister, I do not have that brother- sister relationship with any of my siblings, out of my will. For many years, I have tried to establish that bond, with my two older and, two younger siblings, only to be rejected by them and, hurt in my trying to pull that love from them that is not there. I love my four siblings, but I realize in my life today, that some people are just not meant to go where God is taking you and, some relationships you will have to walk away from, for your own peace of mind and, health. There are some relationships that you will never be able to mend and, it's okay, we have to deal with some people and, family members, from where they are, love them from afar and, keep moving forward with your life. We have no time to sit around crying and, mourning over these broken relationships, we got other things in our own lives that we need to focus on. God has work for us to do, for the kingdom of God, say your prayers for your broken family members and, others and, continue to do the work that we need to do within ourselves, for our own healings. When God removes people from your lives, don't go back and, open up the doors that God has closed to them, for a reason!. One of my friends used to say, pain is a motivator! Meaning we should take from that hurt and, pain to strive! To win bigger! And, aim higher! For ourselves. Don't focus on the then, but let's focus on what we can achieve now! It's a new day! To start all over fresh! Again!, it's never too late to do so.

I pray that through your courage and, enduring strength of God, that I am able to help other victim's of physical and, sexual abuse, to not hold on to the pains and, hurt of being victimized. Remember we are overcomers! And, with Christ as head of our lives, we can get through this and, still live out the goals, dreams, visions and, plans that you want for your life, your future at hand. Today, I thank God! Through it all, I am free! In Christ and, healed! From my traumatic past!. Amen!

If you know someone who may be suffering in silence and, they are showing some signs of mental or emotional instability, please take out the time to see if anything may be going on with them. Whether it be your daughter, son, sister, brother, grandchildren, cousin, aunt, uncle, niece, nephew or friend whomever. Take the time to find out if they may be going through anything and, if they may need some medical or psychiatric support.

Remember, people camouflage well, (I did) they hide behind these smiley faces, (I did for years) and, deep down inside they may be suffering and, crying inside for help, you just don't know. We as a people, a family, have to do better at communicating with each other, supporting and, loving one another. Sometimes all it takes is a simple hug, embrace, or just pick up a phone and, check on your loved ones sometimes and, ask them how are they doing? Or do they need anything? It's just that simple to do.

So, many of us act as if they are so busy, remember that life is not promised to any of us. This world of many people, is lacking God's unconditional love, and, so many don't even know how to define intimacy outside of the physical act itself. Almost everything with this young generation is based around some form of sexual contact. It's like some of our young people have made their bodies, some type of collateral deal now, if I do this for you, what are you going to give me in return for that?.

My goodness, sex, drugs, alcohol, money and, satanic worship is taking over our young people today. This is a time where we all need to be on our hands and, knees to God praying for our loved ones, daily and, praying over our own lives too. We need more love and, concern for each other, spreaded around this world. Without us having a personal relationship with Christ, sharing God's unconditional love and, word with each other, we as a people will stay lost in the darkness of this world.

This is such a dangerous, disrespectful, satanic and stiff necked!, Generation, all you gotta do is, look around you, look at the news and, look at the condition of our families, social environments and, the story will tell itself. Take the time to read Genesis Ch. 19 Vs. 1-29 and, it will give you the details as to why God decided to destroy Sodom and, Gomorrah. God destroyed everyone and, everything there, with fire and, brimstone from heaven, except for Lot and his family. Everyone, even the children, were evil and, wicked in the eyes of the Lord. They were committing all kinds of acts of violence, murder, theft, adultery, fornication, idol worshiping, lying, incest, unnatural sex acts, all kinds of sinful behaviors. Just like what is happening in our world today and, God destroyed them all! Because of their sin!. Not just because of homosexuality and, lesbianism, like people said, no it was because of their sinful behaviors and, them turning away from God!. This is how serious God feels about sin.

Remember God told Noah to build the Ark and, to take his family and, one of each animal in a set, birds, bugs, all walking and, slithering things, that would follow them into the Ark that he and, his family had built. God destroyed all human life and, the animals left on the lands, by water, the great floods from heaven and, the earth, to start creation all over again. Why? Were all of the people destroyed?. They were all destroyed, because they were all wicked, rebellious, evil and, living an immoral lifestyle, and the people turned away from the Lord. Read, Genesis Ch. 6, 7 and, go further on to chapter 8, that talks about the flood and, after the flood was over. What do you believe is coming next, for this generation at hand?. And, most importantly, do you have your life in order and, fully, submitted to Christ, for when God returns to Rapture up, the saints of God and, for the last and, final time, to judge and, condemn all the non-believers of Christ?. If you have just an inch of doubt, that you do not know, if you are going to heaven or hell, when you die, then you quickly! Need to repent of your sins, right now, not later! And, fully, submit your life to Christ and, your children and, loved ones too. Amen!.

CHAPTER 4

It's Like Sleeping With The Enemy- Defeat Them With Your Prayers.

BY THE AGE of twenty three, I now had three small children to raise, my second child was my princess daughter and, my third and, special last born, my youngest son. By now, I had been through so, much with my siblings, family and, friends that I didn't really trust anyone in my life at all. It seemed like I was taking care of everyone's needs but my own. I was supporting my two younger siblings, nieces, nephews and, my mother, even moving them in with me and, my daughters father, when things got rough for them. I had helped a few of my younger cousins and, friends who needed a place to stay and, financially, supported my family as well.

I had totally lost myself, my identity, in the negativity, toxic lifestyles, arguments and, fights between us all throughout the years. It just continued to get worse as my life moved on. We all had been in a couple of shelters for women and, children back then, due to having a lack of income, to pay rent and, bills and, me leaving the abusive relationship that I was in. Everywhere that I went or moved, I took my mother and, two younger siblings with me. I found myself trying to be the mother and, father that my sister and, younger brother never had. Even though my mother was present, mentally she was not, she had no knowledge as to how to live her life, on her own, without her children caring for her physical needs. But, it was okay, because me and, my sister wanted nothing more than to take care of our mothers every need since she had been so abused by our father, most of her life. Not to mention, we don't know all of the things that my mother suffered, as a young girl throughout her childhood, with her family members. But, there was some abuse.

My oldest brother, as I said, had joined the Navy, fresh out of highschool, to get away from our fathers abuse. Once he left, we didn't see him again, until maybe twenty years down the line, maybe only once then. He had moved away after the Military, started his own family and, completely erased us all from his life, for almost twenty years. My next oldest brother had moved out of the house, by the age of twelve as I said, earlier, with his best friend's family and, then he left Chicago later, as he became an adult. He also started his own family and, we only saw him maybe once, every five years or more and, he was only a three hour car ride away. He also erased all of us, for many, many years out of his life, the same way that my oldest brother did, when he left home. All my mother, my sister, her children and, my youngest brother had to look up to was me, the middle child and, I had three children to raise alone, all while fighting in an abusive relationship at that time, with my children's father. I hate how we allow the enemy to divide our families and, we won't take the time out to communicate with each other. We have so much arrogance! And, pride! About ourselves, that we can't make the time to support and, love each other, as Christ loves us. Our family is supposed to be the ones that you can lean on, for anything in your time of need, but, unfortunately you will get more help from a friend, than your own family.

I know many of you, may have had parents that may have been incompetent, of caring for you and, your siblings and, you were forced to spend your childhood or young adolescent years, caring for your siblings or a parent on your own.

So, I know you can understand the heavy load, stress, exhaustion and, fear that I had, during my teens and, twenties, with no help or financial support from anyone. Everyone depends on you to take care of their needs, when you have nothing but God to depend on to help you mentally, emotionally and, physically to get through.

I had spent five years with my children's father, who was a severe alcoholic and, I was beaten by him throughout those horrible five years, almost every other day. I had become my mother, in a younger version all over again. My mother's abuse was something that I did not want in my own life, to become an abused spouse, like she was for years, with my father. That same victim of physical, mental and, emotional abuse, I had become a reflection of my mother, in my relationships with men, with no voice.

I can remember when myself, my two older brothers and, my sister were young, my mother would sit and, have conversations with herself, as if someone was sitting and, talking to her. Some of the things that she spoke, you could understand, but the majority of the things she said were scattered words, as she also laughed to herself. She would be picking the cotton from blankets and, shirts until holes formed and, uncontrollably, she would start laughing to herself for no reason at all.

It was scary for me, from the age of twelve throughout my teenage years, seeing my mother laugh and, talk out loud to herself. None of us understood what was wrong with my mommy, whom her children loved so much. My father would laugh at my mother, when she talked to herself and, tell us that she was crazy and, that she had demons in her.

I knew that my mother needed psychological mental help, and, as a child, I had no power to help my mother and, she had no family in the city to help her as well. I believed through the stress of the abuse from my father, her raising five children, with barely enough to survive off, when my father would leave, for days with his mistresses, all of this mentally affected my mother. Also, being taken away from her mother and, her family by my father and, his mother to Chicago, so young, without her mother's consent back then. All of that played a heavy role on my mother's mental capacity. I knew, as I got older, that my mother was also suffering from some form of undiagnosed mental health disorder, because she had siblings and, relatives with mental health disorders as well.

When my father left my mother, amazingly, she did completely stop talking to herself out loud and, laughing out loud as she was doing everyday. But, I know that my mother does suffer from some form of mental health disorder and, I pray that one-day, my sister, who has my mother, with her five children, gets my mother the psychological help that she needs at seventy, one years young now. During the years that I suffered physical and, mental abuse at the hands of my children's father, I remember back one-day, my children's father cracked my head open, with a vase that stood high up to your knees. It was very heavy to lift, from the floor and, I remember standing in my front room talking to my mother, sister, my sister's oldest daughter's father, who was visiting her and, my baby brother. They were sitting on the coach, as I stood talking about something to them. My children's father had come home drunk as always and, I paid him no mind and, I continued talking to my family. Next thing I know, I heard a crash! And, I felt a pain from the top of my head, as blood rolled down my forehead.

I grabbed my head dazed, wobbly and, in shock, I could not believe he had injured me this way, right in front of my family, as they were sitting there. He had walked behind me, picked up the vase and, he crashed! The heavy vase, on top of my head, for no reason at all. Mind you my family was sitting in front of me and, they could see him, as he had picked up the vase. Did any of them scream out! And, warn me to move, because he had picked up that vase, no they didnt. Did anyone jump up! From the coach and, defend me or attack him, after he slammed! The vase over my head, absolutely not!.

They all just sat there, as I ran and, grabbed my phone and, a towel for my bleeding head, calling the police to come and, arrest him. Had that been my sister, getting hit over the head with a large, floor vase that way, I would have tore! The whole house up! With him! For hurting my sister that way. Me and, him would have been pretty, beat up! Together! Before the police arrived to arrest him! I tell you that.

But not one of them said a word to him in my defense, it was five of us against only one of him and, he was very drunk. Together we all could have taken him down and, gave him a good butt! Whipping! Before the police got there. But as always throughout my life, there was no one to speak up in my defense or help me through my life struggles. The police came and, he had left of course by then, the police took me to the hospital not that far away and, I received about ten stitches in the top of my scalp. Mind you, I had my family living there with me, until they got their own place to live. As I said earlier, everywhere I moved, my family followed me as well. My sister and, my brother were around nineteen or twenty, when this particular assault happened to me, in front of them.

When I made it back home, he came back home later that night, as if nothing had ever happened. I showed him my stitches in my head and, he did not apologize, or show any signs of concern, not sympathy, for nearly killing! Me with that floor vase. My three children were in their room, feets away from me, when their father cracked my head open that day, to my skull!.

That was one of many wounds that I suffered at my children's father's hands. My arm had been fractured by him, while I was six months pregnant with our daughter and, he had fractured the right side of my ribs, while I was about seven months pregnant with our daughter. My daughter was born with a large lump on her chest, over her heart and, my baby had to be put on oxygen, immediately after she was born. She had complications breathing and, I cried trying to see her from the birthing table, because I thought my precious, baby daughter was going to die from the knot on her chest. When I asked the doctors, could it have come from the physical abuse that I had suffered, from being beaten, often while I was pregnant with her, by her father and, the doctor told me, that it was a possibility, yes. As I told you earlier, I was a child, who had already been abused from my mother's womb, by the abuse from the hands of my father, afflicting my mother. Now, here I was, a reflection of my mother, being beaten by my children's father and, my daughter being born, abused just like I was from the womb, my baby, being born with a large bruise, a lump right over her heart. Those patterns and, cycles of physical and, emotional abuse that I spoke about earlier, I had become a victim of the same abusive cycle, and, patterns of my abused mother, some of my abused aunties, some of my abused cousins and, many of my abused friends that I had grown up with. Now, I had birth a child into the world, who had already become a victim of abuse, at the hands of her father, that she had never known, as her father. You see the cycles here that I spoke about?.

Furthermore, I thanked God! That my baby was okay. After a few days of the doctor monitoring the lump, her tiny heart and, my daughter's breathing, the lump went away in time and, I brought my baby home, safely.

Her father came to the hospital a few hours after she was born, picking our baby up and, kissing her all over her face, like a proud father would. All I could do was watch him holding our baby at the hospital and, wonder if he was the cause of us almost losing our daughter after birth, from his physical abuse towards me, during the pregnancy. Right then, I should have left him, but, unfortunately with no place to go, I didn't.

My children's father, family members and, friends knew that he was beating me, because he had beaten me at his brother's house one-day at his house party, in front of him and, his friends one-day. I was severely beaten at one of his sisters' apartments one-day as well, when we were visiting her. Both of my eyes were closed shut and, I had a severe brain concussion, from the beating that day. He nearly beat me to death, in front of his nieces that day, out of one of his crazed! Drunken days, for no reason at all. Ask me if anyone jumped in to fight him in my defense, with lots of others around, during the assaults at his brother and, sisters house, and, the answer is no!.

No one ever came to my rescue to save or defend me for anything. Everytime I looked in the mirror at my swollen, closed eye or busted lip, I saw my mother over and, over again and, I hated it. I had nowhere to go, with three small kids and, no income just like my mothers situation back then and, that was why I continued to stay with him, as long as I did, for five years.

There were many days that my mother had a black eye and, busted up lip, at the hands of my father when I was a child. She didn't have anyone to defend or protect her either, some of my father's siblings and, my grandmother knew that my father was beating up my mother.

Maybe they could have helped to send my mother back home to Mississippi, on the Greyhound bus to her mother and, five brothers that she had. She had not seen her mother and, brother's in over twenty years, during that time. That could have easily been done, by his family, helping to send my mother back home, because my mother did want to go back home to her mother, before she died. Mentally my mother didn't know how to leave my father, on her own with five kids at that time who were little and, mentally she was not stable enough to find her way back to her family by herself.

If you know that someone is being abused or harmed and, you turn your head with a blind eye and, do nothing to help that person, you are just as bad as the abuser is!. And, you will have to give account for your non-accountability to God, for not helping as a mandated reporter, concerning someone you know, that is being abused. That's just my take on it. If you hear something, see something and, you know that something is wrong, SAY! SOMETHING! You could be saving somebody's life for God's sake!. In most families, we like to brush everything under the rug and, tell eachother what happens or goes on in the house, stays in the house. Where the heck! Did that lie come from? Who made that up and, wrote that in stone to stay quiet and, hide abuse or sexual abuse within the family home?.

This is still happening, sad to say, in many homes today, where family members hide abuse. Do you know how many women, young girls, young boys and, men die at the hands of their abusers, because no one wanted to intervene or help them?. We have this mentality or attitude about the situation like, well it's none of my business or why don't they just leave? And, I ain't got nothing to do with it. But if you know about it and, have witnessed someone being abused, you are now a part of it, yes, you are! And, you need to report what you have seen or know to the proper authorities. You can report crimes anonymously as well, without giving a name or your personal information. There are hotlines toll free, that anyone can call, to report any kind of crime.

A lot of victims like I did for years, they stay in abusive situations, because they don't have family support, no money and, nowhere to go, especially if the woman has children. You feel trapped as if no one cares if you're dead or alive, and, you convince yourself to stay. A lot of women do, for the sake of the kids, having a place to live.

If you have never walked in the shoes of a person who has been victimized by someone, you have no right to judge them or throw your rocks! At them, because you don't know or understand their (My) story.

I'm sure there are some of you, who have suffered from domestic or sexual abuse, as I have and, I only pray, that you are not in that situation today and, that you have gotten the counseling and, therapy that you may need as I received. There is nothing wrong with seeking counseling and, psychiatric help, to help you cope with the abuse that you have endured. The worst part is continuing to suffer from the trauma, from your abuse in silence and, not going to get the help that you may need to heal and, move forward with your life and, goals.

Some people may even require medication, to help them focus and, overcome from depression, anxiety, panic attacks and, PTSD. I myself did not get the proper treatment that I needed for my trauma, until ten years ago. I am so glad that I finally woke up, after suffering in silence for years and, got a proper diagnosis from my primary care doctor and, psychiatrist as well. I needed to be on medication to help me overcome the trauma that I endured throughout my childhood and, adolescent years of physical, sexual and, emotional abuse.

The medications have done wonders for me and, have allowed me to be able to focus, sleep and, function at a normal level in my life today. I am grateful that I finally got the right doctors to help support my mental needs, to God! I give him all the praise!. I still see my doctors and, therapist today, continuing to take my medications for my mental health needs.

You can do nothing in your life for you or your family, if your mental health is not good, it is a crippling and, debilitating position to be in. Trying to deal with your trauma alone is not easy to do and, you can mentally burn out! (I did). If you are suffering with your mental health, I plead with you to love yourself and, family enough, to seek the right medical doctors that can help you, get the right medical treatments that work for your mental health needs. If you are in an abusive relationship with anyone, please seek someone that you trust and, ask them to help you get out of that house or situation with that person or people. Your life and, children matter and, you don't want to lose your life at the hands of an abuser or continue to be harmed.

There are a lot of programs available today that can help anyone suffering from any form of domestic abuse and, violence. You can contact here in Illinois 211, 311, 611, the police 911 or The Department of Human Services for mental health services, low income program information and, shelter placement ect. Reach out to family, friends or even church organizations if you can, but do whatever you can in secret, without the abuser knowing your moves to leave. Do everything that you can safely, to get out of that situation as quickly as you can. I pray that I have been a support here for anyone going through physical or mental abuse by an abuser.

CHAPTER 5

Sometimes I Feel Like A Crab In A Barrel- But The Transition Moves Forward.

AFTER I HAD suffered from so many years of abuse and, trauma I went back to school and, got my license in nursing, at a trade school, by the age of twenty four. I wanted to get a job, working in the hospitals, to get a place for me and, my children to call home. I realized that I had to help myself, get up and, make it happen, because no one was coming to our rescue. It was up to me to save myself and, my children from homelessness.

My sister later followed my lead, after I told her to also go back to school and, to get her a certificate in patient care at that time and, she did. I had met a new love, a guy who was six years older than me, with no kids, who was working as a security guard, at one of the shelters that me and, my children and, family were placed in. Olive Branch Shelter, I will never forget by, Western Ave here in Chicago, it was our temporary place to call home and, we had met a couple of good women with kids there too.

I had mustered up enough strength to finally leave my children's father, after almost five years of vicious beatings!. I packed up two, large shoulder bags of clothes one morning. I grabbed my babies by the hand, when their father went out, I fled with my youngest son in my arms and, the other two kids at my side running. We were running down the block to a bus stop, two blocks away from my house, as I was waving down the bus coming, so terrified, for the bus approaching us, to stop, in fear that their father may be near and, catch me trying to leave with them. Praise God! We made it on that bus, that was the beginning of me being free! From my children's father's physical, mental and, emotional abuse!. It was over!.

We went to a police station and, they called for the women's shelter to come and, get us, after a twelve hour wait, in the hallway of the police station, sitting in these hard, plastic chairs. Of course my mother, sister and, brother came there with me to the shelter. We were all there together as a family in the shelter, and, we bounced around from shelter to shelter, until we were able to get our own place to live. My sister took my mother with her and, her baby, she now had and, I took my brother with me during that time.

I had moved around to three different places, and my brother brought along with him three different young ladies, throughout his stays with me, during those years and, their children. Unfortunately, none of them stayed long with him, because my brother turned out to be just like my father at nineteen or twenty years young, beating up on his girlfriends and, he was also, a heavy, young alcoholic. My second oldest brother, he had a history of fighting women too, one dark part in his life and, he also became a heavy drinker, just like our father. These are the cycles and, patterns that I have been talking about, within the family generation.

Just as I said before, whatever your children grow up seeing in their home, amongst parents, or peers, in their social environment, negative or positive, that is how many children grow up and, behave towards themselves and, others. Two brothers out of my three brothers, took on my father's abusive behavior that he had towards my mother and, his addiction to alcohol.

Some of you reading my book may have even had moments in your life, where you became the worst part of abusive parents or peers in your life, growing up. It can happen to even the best of people, that you would never have believed that they took a dark path in life, due to their social environment that they were raised in, throughout their childhood.

Also, there are some people who didn't come from abusive homes, believe it or not, and, some of those same people, took a wrong path in life and, it cost them everything! As well. They may have hung around the wrong type of people, who were living careless and, dangerous lives. Or some people may have experienced some form of crisis that hit them in their life and, they just couldn't recover from that trauma.

They may have made the wrong decisions and, choices to cope, by turning to drugs, alcohol, pills, sexual perversions with multiple partners and, even suffered from a mental disorder, that was hereditary through their family generation. It's not just people who have come from abusive homes that take the wrong paths in life, it can happen to just about anyone in their life, depending on the situations that you may face.

When I decided to go back to school to get some type of certificate under my belt, it helped me feel like I was somebody and, that I did matter in this world. I had three, growing children who were depending on me to take care of all of their needs, since their father was no longer in the house.

When we were together, he did watch the kids, when I needed to take care of business, their father even cooked dinners on a lot of his sober, good days. And, he was a heck of a good house cleaner too, he had a lot of good qualities that I did love about him, similar to my father's good traits.

When I first met my children's father, he would buy me these fancy dresses, because I was young, and, beautiful as a teenager. Once we moved in together, he took me around all his family and, friends showing me off. We loved to go out to different lounges across the city dancing and, enjoying the night together. My kids' father protected me from anyone who may have tried to harm me and, honestly, I felt my safest with our kids, when I traveled with him. He gave me money, whenever I needed it, when he did odd jobs and, surprisingly, he would give me almost his whole check to help pay the bills.

I fell in love with my children's father as a young teenager, because no one had ever treated me this way and, showed this type of love and, care for me. He didn't start out a monster! An abuser, but this is what you call "Grooming" and, pulling your victim in. Groomers know the type of victims that they can control, they normally prey on the weak, vulnerable, nieve and, lonely victim's.

They seek out the ones who they feel have low self-esteem about themselves and, have no family that cares about them. I was the perfect package that fit that list and, he knew it well, when he met me at his sister's apartment, who lived in the same building that me and, my family was living in.

This is the reason why I stayed so, many years in the abuse, I had never been wined and, dined the way my children's father came in the door treating me. He made me feel so protected and, loved and, honestly, my children's father loved me in his own way. He still does even today, now that our children are grown, I forgave him by God's grace many years ago and we are good friends today. But, at that time of the abuse, he had no clue how to treat me, love me unconditionally and, protect me even from himself. He too came from an abusive childhood, where he and, most of his siblings were adopted and, separated from each other in foster care. My children's father told me how they all suffered in their childhood life, by foster parents.

Even when I left my children's father for good, when my daughter was about four or five, I never stopped my children's father from having a relationship with his children. We had made peace and, I would allow him when he was sober, to come to our house and, spend hours with his children. When I needed him to help me with our children when I was sick and, needed a babysitter for the kids, my children's father was there at the blink of an eye, supporting me with the help of our children.

Financially, he could not help me, because of his addiction to alcohol, he could not mentally or physically hold down any job. But, as far as his presence in our children's lives, despite what he had done to me, I wanted my children to have a relationship with their father. I never talked bad about my children's father to them, because of the abuse he did to me, because it had nothing to do with them. I did not want to poison them, against having some type of relationship with their father. I invited him to all the birthday parties that I had for them, to Thanksgiving dinners and, Christmas dinners that I had to. He came over even in the presence of my two previous husbands at the time. They welcomed my children's father to come and, celebrate with us and, his children. I had an understanding with my spouse and, they did not mind me allowing my children's father to come over and, spend those holidays and, birthdays with us. To this day, now that our children are grown, with their own kids, they are now allowing him to spend time with their children, his grandchildren, despite the fact that he is still a severe alcoholic even today. I poured the love of God's unconditional love within my children. I did this, so that they could look past their fathers sickness and, to just love him for who he was in their lives and, that he was their father first!.

I hate to see some women stop the child or children from having a relationship with their father, because of whatever kind of circumstances went on between them. Or because he has no job to support the children. Now, if it's a matter, where it endangers the mothers life or the children, I understand that, the courts of law should be involved, to work out that situation. But, if a mother is keeping a father away from his children out of spite, anger that he moved on or because he has no money, that is wrong and, only hurts the children involved. Those children having a father present in their life, is far more important to me, because there are too many negative and, dangerous things going on in this world today and, children need that father's presence to help talk to them about life and, to help guide them along their lives, if the father is fit to lead his children.

Father's have the right to still see their children and, even get the courts involved, so that he can get visitation rights, to see and, take his children on scheduled court ordered weekends or holidays, however it works for both adults parties. None of my friends had fathers in their homes and, they were very angry and, got caught up in a lot of serious issues throughout their life. I had a father present who was abusive to my mother, but his presence kept me and, my siblings at that time out of the streets and, doing a lot of harmful stuff. Whatever you pour into your children, that is how they will behave as they get older. Children need to grow up seeing love, proper communication, morals, values and, good discipline being modeled by the adults in their lives and, within their environment. I pray that you, my readers, are taking notes here and, will apply some of those same healthy values within your children, marriage and, family structure. Our children deserve love, they did not ask to be brought into this world. As parents it is our responsibility to raise our children with healthy values, morals, discipline and, with a loving and, safe environment throughout their life, teaching them also about the love of God!.

Do you see the pattern here that I am writing out? Everyone that I have spoken about so far, who suffered from some form of abuse or addiction in their upbringing, were themselves raised in an abusive family upbringing, in their childhood. And, mind you, everyone that I knew, or dealt with and, hung around, throughout my life, had suffered from some type of physical, mental and, emotional abuse in their life. Oftentimes, you will find that many, victims of domestic abuse, or have parents on drugs and relatives, tend to cling to others like them, who they feel can relate to what they are going through.

Some people say that within families, this is called generational curses. If I see one more video of these false!, Fake! Prophets and Prophetesses, on YouTube, Tic Toc and, Instagram, proha-lying! That people are suffering in their life, from family generational curses, I'm going to scream!.

Jesus Christ, the sacrificial Lamb, who paid the price, for mankind's sins at the cross on calvary, died for our sins at the cross. If curses still exist, then why don't we just go back to sacrificing lambs and, goats on an altar, everytime that we believe that we have sinned. If Jesus Christ paid the price at the cross, for all of mankind's sins, why would any of us be still attached to generational curses today?. In the scriptures it reads in, Galatians Ch. 3: Vs. 13-14 it reads, [13] Christ hath redeemed us from the curse of the law, being made a curse for us: for it is written, Cursed is everyone that hangeth on a tree: [14] That the blessing of Abraham might come on the Gentiles through Jesus Christ; that we might receive the promise of the Spirit through faith. Amen!

Through Christ we are free of the law and, any curses, we are now under grace! In the new testament. Aren't you glad as I am, that Jesus Christ died on the cross so that we can have salvation, which is free! To all of mankind?. That's how much Jesus Christ loves each and, everyone of us and, God wants us to live for eternity with him, when we leave this body, here on earth. He is a faithful God to his word and, promises unto us and, God is a God that cannot! Tell a lie and, go back on his word!. Man, woman, boy or girl will lie to you, decieve you, betray you, harm you and, let you down, but my father in heaven, our Lord never! Ever Will. If you don't have a personal relationship with Christ, please do so and, experience his healing power and, love as I have, surrendering my life over to God many years ago. Will you still have challenges in life that we all will face? Yes, but with Jesus Christ in your life, he will give you the strength and, comfort to get through it. Amen!

So, as I was saying earlier, I went back to college and received a license in nursing to take care of my family and, I had met a new love in my life, from the shelter. I fell head over heels in love with this man, because he truly cared for all the women and, children in the shelter. He did everything that he could, to take care of our needs while we were living there with our children. My family and, I became very close with him after a few months of getting to know him, when we would go outside to the park, up the street with our kids. Soon, he started inviting me to come visit him at his small, box room, studio unit near downtown. We had to hide it from the staff that we were dating and, from other clients at the shelter, because if they knew that he was dating a client at the shelter, he could be terminated on the spot!.

No staff were allowed to date any of the women or men at the shelter period. He was a very, skinny, dark skinned guy, around thirty years young, to my twenty four years young. He was fairly handsome, weird, but funny at the same time. And, a lot of other young girls at the shelter and, some of the women staff were attracted to him too. One of the girls who had two small kids, had become very close to me and, my sister. One night, she told him, as she was sitting across from my bed talking to me, that I liked him, when he came to my bed to tell us it was time to shut the floor down for bed. We all slept in this big room, with twin beds lined up in a row, on each side of the two long walls. And, he sat at a desk at the end of the hall, at night, watching over the two units of us women and, children.

How would I ever have known, from meeting such a gentle and, caring man, that I had met another badly, broken and, damaged young man. His lifestyle and, abusive behavior was far worse than my children's father, but, without the physical abuse. It was more mental and, emotional abuse that I suffered the most by him. After I had gotten attached with him, even my family, along with my three children, a year or so later, was when he finally started telling me some serious, personal things about himself and, his family, which was very dark. He was from New York City and, he had been residing in Chicago only for a few years. When he started to confess his past life with me, I was so furious at him, for waiting all of this time, to tell me about a lot of things that he had done and, been through. I remembered jumping up from his bed as we were laying together talking. I asked him why he didn't tell me these things long ago about himself and, he seemed clueless to my question. He basically told me that he felt I needed to know everything about his life, to free his guilt, of holding certain things back, from me. I was crushed and, shocked, because I felt like he had lied to me and, betrayed my trust that I thought I had found in him. I didn't know he had a severe drug and, alcohol addiction, or that he had spent half of his life in and, out of the penitentiary and, other things that I will not talk about here. He had multiple felonies on his criminal record history and, he came from a family, being raised by abusive parents, siblings, aunts and, uncles who had very, dark lifestyles of addiction, abuse and so, on.

My heart had become so in tune with him, that I didn't have the strength in me, after leaving my children's father to let him go. I thought in my heart, that I had finally found that true, unconditional love of God, that I was searching for all of my life, in a mate. My family loved him and, my children had grown to love him, so, I forgave him for holding some major things back from me, about his past and, his life. I know many of you know that was the wrong thing to do. Why? Did I brush it all under the rug?. It was because of the brokenness! Within me and, as I said, earlier, familiar spirits tend to find each other somehow. All I knew, or had been around my entire life, was broken and, damaged people, who were living just as I was, out of the will of God. Not one person that I knew of hung around, went to church, had a good family relationship, or had a personal relationship with God and, they didn't want a life in Christ either.

When I tell you this relationship took me down some of the darkest roads of my life, I don't think words could even explain it all. I married him, despite the fact that he was in and, out of prison most of our relationship. Every few months after he would get out of prison, from doing three, four, five and, seven years of incarcerations, over and, over again, he would ask me to wait for him and, because I loved him that much, I did. Every time he got out of prison, it was back to the years, and, years of turmoil, hurt, pain, suffering, lies, manipulation, mental and, emotional abuse, gaslighting, his alcohol addiction, his drug addictions and, years of cheating. All the years of betrayal I tell you, completely traumatize my soul!. I could add more traumatic words here, but I think you get the just, of what kind of man, that I married and, I had stayed twenty five years with off and on, as my children had become adults.

I know many of you are probably thinking, how is she still sane in her right mind today, after all of these traumatic experiences, that has happened to her?. Yes, I get it I know, I wondered for many years, asking myself the same question too. Some days I wondered if I was even breathing? Because for a lot of days, I was hardly breathing from my pain. I was going through the motions of functioning like a normal person, but, inside I was barely breathing and, living. I was just a programmed robot, doing the things that I was programmed to do and, say.

My boyfriend, who is my husband today, did not have a job when we moved into our own place after leaving the shelter life and, my sister and, mother had got their own place as well. He was fired from the shelter where we met, because he told the director of the shelter that he was going to marry me. He had gotten me this cheap two, hundred dollar ring that I adored and, he told all the staff and, women that we were going to get married. He did not want to hide our relationship anymore he said, but all the staff and, women knew of our love and, were so happy for us as well.

When I got the apartment for us, we were exhausted mentally from being homeless for so long. We had stayed a few months with my grandmother, in her basement, me, him, my kids, my brother and, his girlfriend at the time. And, we even lived with my father in his old, dirty basement apartment that he was renting for a couple of months during that time, before we finally had our own place to call home.

I had gotten a job working at a nursing home, five blocks away from my building, I barely made enough to keep the rent, light, gas, cable and, phone bill paid. I had helped my brother to get on disability and, he was giving me half his check, to help me pay the rent, since I let his girlfriend move in with us, from the shelter.

I used whatever food stamps that I got to keep food in the house, which they weren't giving me much, because I was working. The government didn't care that I was making below poverty level, in income and, that all of my income went towards the rent and, bills. All the government did for a mother with children, who had a job was give you a handful of food stamps, to help you feed your children and, a medical card, to at least go to the doctor with your children.

Even though I had a full time job and, I was getting help from my brother, I was still struggling to stay afloat. My rent was nine hundred dollars a month, for a big, three bedroom apartment, that had a huge living room and, day porch that was walking distance from the beach. That was actually cheap back then, because today, an apartment that size, with three bedrooms near the beach, would cost you nearly four to five thousand dollars a month for sure, here in Chicago. But, in the late 80s and, 90s these big, huge apartments on the Eastside and, Southside of Chicago, the rent was dirt cheap!. The apartments had these huge living rooms and, dining rooms included in these big, court way apartment buildings back then and, you never paid over nine hundred dollars, for these twelve and, thirteen hundred, square feet apartments back then.

Those days are long gone now, a one bedroom apartment today will cost you around fourteen hundred dollars a month, depending on what area of the city you live in and, it could cost even more, if you lived in a gated community. You need about two to three steady incomes, just to survive here in this expensive city today. I know how hard it is for single mothers, who are working and, going to school, to get ahead in life. It is not easy, if you have no support from a working father in the home, or a father who is paying child support to take care of his kids. I was that mother throughout my children's life, having no financial support from their father or anyone, to help me with the rent and, bills. My husband, who was my boyfriend back then, never helped me to pay any bills, because he was either running the streets, getting high, with loose women, whomever, or he was in and, out of prison. Even within the marriage, he financially was not helping me with the bills. My husband won a lawsuit within our relationship and then marriage after twenty years together by then, while he was in prison, due to him being beaten up by prison guards. He put the money, in a female friend of his account, that he knew and, had her to send me twelve thousand dollars, of his thirty thousand dollar settlement. That was the only money he had ever given me, the twenty five years that I stuck by his side and, supported him through his many incarcerations and, his in and, out of rehabilitation center for alcohol and, drug use. I was there with him, through everything that he went through, as his girlfriend and, wife and, each time he got home. But, it was constant verbal and, mental abuse that I suffered by him and, he could not love me, or be loyal to me, the way that I was to him. He could not give me what he, himself didn't have and, that was unconditional love, loyalty nor respect for me as his wife. He was broken and, living this destructive lifestyle, way before I even existed to him, this was who he was from a child growing up, in an abusive home. He had been living in the streets, he told me, since the age of twelve, so he had no real morals or family values that had been taught to him. Even though I was a single mother, I was raised knowing what those family values were, by my peers within the Church family, that I grew up around during my childhood. And, I did have a personal relationship with Christ living within me, so, I was never, really like the people that I surrounded myself around.

Single mothers get a bad rap, from others looking in from the outside, belittling them, for having no father in the home, that was providing for their children. They would say, things like, she knew that he wasn't nothing or not capable of taking care of children, when she met him, so, that is her fought for having kids with him. Well in some situations that may be true, but in many cases it is not.

I know a lot of women, who were in relationships and, marriages with men, who had a job and, were providers. But, once the relationship or marriage was over, those father's abandoned their children. Many of those men didn't want to pick their children up for visits and, the women had to file child support, because the father did not want to take financial care of the child, (Or children) once the relationship was over.

It's not just women, who have kids by incompetent men, who have suffered from the father not supporting his child or children by the mother, no. There are thousands of mother's, of all races and, ethnicities of people, who will tell you some of the same stories. The father of their children, who had a job, in the home, completely abandoned their child, or children, physically and, financially once the relationship or marriage was over.

So, those people who judge single women, who are raising a child or children alone, need to stop bashing! These great, single mothers. Many of these women are out there working, not asking for handouts and, even going to school, to take care of their children and, home. If you have never walked in their shoes (My) then keep your negative comments and, thoughts to yourself, until you know both sides of the story first!.

We all have made some bad decisions and, choices in our lives that we can't change. Lord knows I have and, I am telling it all, right here in this book, openly without shame. If I could do it all over again, I know, I would not have trusted some of the people and, family members that I allowed into my life back then. I would have ran! The other way from them, but, I take full accountability for the poor choices and, decisions that I myself made and, I am not pointing the finger at anyone.

My foolery! And, poor choices that I myself made, have cost me years of my life, that I cannot ever get back. But, is it over for me or you, who have awakened from our mishaps in life? No! It's not too late to reinvent yourself. You can pick yourself up, get out of that depression, sadness, blame pointing and, procrastination spirit of the enemy and, start from where you are at. You (We) still are breathing air and, hopefully in your right mind, with good health and, we can still start a new, fresh path again! With Christ guiding us through. The only person that can stop you, from moving forward and, doing a new thing in your life, right now, today is you! (Us). Okay, let me get back to the story.

Throughout my years with my husband, there were dozens of women that my husband had cheated on me with, as I stayed faithful, loyal and, committed to him in our marriage. I was there with him, when he was fired from his job, for admitting that we were together in the shelter where we met.

I stood by his side, took up for him in his wrongs and, supported him, when he had nothing! And, Nobody but me, my children and, my family by his side. My family accepted him, because of the love that I had for him and, my grandmother (RIP) my father (RIP) and, my mother cared for him as a father cared for a son. They never judged my husband or put him down to me or anyone that we knew and, they knew he was not treating me right. Every time I waited for him to get home from prison, I sent money to his commissary at the prison, sent hundreds of letters, magazines and, puzzle books that he loved, through his many years of incarceration. Mind you, I was barely making enough money to survive on my own, with my children and, paying rent and, bills

I spent hundreds of dollars through the years, on those expensive phone calls from prison, that were like twenty five dollars, for six calls only, taking money from my bills and, my children's needs, to support him. Not to forget, I was paying a hundred and, fifty dollars at a time, to ride on the buses that took families out of state, to go and, visit their loved ones in prison. I did this for years, trying to be there and, help to save a man, my boyfriend, then husband, that didn't even want to save himself!.

It was a sad, lonely feeling, being on the loaded van or bus, with other broken women like myself, going to visit our loved ones in prison. We were all victims and, prisoners in some form of way, with them, because our life was constantly interrupted, by being slaves to their addictions, brokenness of their destructive behavior and, lifestyle that we didn't live. There were some good days, yes it was, when my husband was sober and, drug free. The days that he would be home with me, and, not in the streets or in prison, I cherished so much.

When he wasn't out in the streets, doing God knows what, all I wanted to do was cook a hot, big meal for us all and, lay in the bed and, watch a few movies with him. I didn't require much, I just wanted that quality time, of intimacy without the sex, to just look at him, smile at him, feed him and, the kids a good meal and, have that family bond that I never had as a child with my parents.

My father was always gone at work day and, night or gone for three to four days, at his mistresses' houses. He came and, went whenever he wanted to, my father did, because my mother had no voice against my father and, what he did when he was gone. When there was no food in the house, during the days that my father was gone, my mother would go to the neighbors house that she knew in our building and, ask them for food for me and, my two, older brothers at the time.

We went hungry many times, because my father would also cash in half of the food stamps that my mother got from AFDC. He would pay off the alcohol, tobacco and, cigarette tabs (Debts) that he had, from the owners of the liquor stores, that he knew and, they trusted my father to pay his tabs every month. My father did small jobs for them, when they needed work done, so, they had no problem letting my father get anything that he wanted, on an "IOU" to pay them off later. But, he would pay them off, with most of my mother's food stamps, that were for her to buy food with every month. The Arab, store owners, would allow my father to get all the alcohol and, tobacco that he wanted every month, in exchange for food stamps, on the first, when my mother picked up the food stamp books from the currency exchange. Women got their cash and, food stamps books, through the currency exchange, every month when it was time for you to get the cash and, food stamps that the government gave you for your children. Sounds like the tomb! Stone! Ages right? Many of you don't know anything about AFDC Welfare, Aid For Dependent Children, in the 70s, 80s and, 90s.

The line would be halfway wrapped around the currency exchange building, with mother's with their children, husband or boyfriend, waiting anxiously, to get their government assistance. Inside the book of food stamps it would be paper ones, fives and, tens, like cash, a dollar bill, five dollar bill or ten dollar bill etc. The food stamps by number, would be a different color, like brown, purple, green, yellow and, blue. Yes, that's what food stamps looked like back in the 60s, 70s and, 80s. Type it in on your phone, to see what food stamp books looked like, during that time for women who received AFDC Welfare. Today, they give the women and, men a plastic like, credit card that has your cash and, food stamp benefits on it to shop with. And, you can call the number on the back of the card, to see how much you have on the card, along with other information they give you, concerning your cash and, food stamps benefits. We've come a long way from the AFDC era right?.

Believe it or not, there are still women who have to sell their food stamps to people they know, or to some Arab store owners who will buy them for cash. There are still women who are working or not working that have to sell their food stamps, so that they can use the extra money for bills and, their children's needs, unfortunately. I don't down or knock women that are forced by lack and, have to sell part of their food stamps to keep a roof over their head. I don't know their situation, struggles or story, so, who am I to judge someone, for what they are doing to survive, for their children and, to pay their rent?.

I used to be just like those women, with my three children trying to stay afloat, so, I know the struggles that many women with children have, who have no family support or father of their children, supporting their children, as I didn't either. That's why I pray, one-day, that families, all races of people, will try to become closer and, more supportive of each other, than many broken families are today, like mine. We are not each other's enemy, as I said, there are real demonic forces that use people to divide the family, children and, spouse against one another. Until we become a better family and, people towards one another, these evil forces will continue to win at destroying our families and, our lives.

During my rollercoaster ride of doom! With my husband, my heart went out to him, I truly loved him and, my husband was brilliant in other ways. My husband could draft out any type of petitions for people, whether it be criminal or for marriage separations, like he was an actual attorney down to the 'T'!.

Anything dealing with the judicial systems, my husband knew it, read and, studied it and, he could draft it out and, explain it in legal terms, as if he was a supreme court judge!. My husband has a brilliant! Mind, but he is badly, broken and, mentally disturbed as well. My husband's childhood traumas, alcohol and, drug addiction of his life, has prevented him from being the best! Man that God created him to be. Even to this day, he has not changed the broken cycles and, patterns of his life, that keeps him hell! Bound! One-day.

I had to learn the hard way that you cannot make any person, get better, do better, or change, unless they want it for themselves. You are wasting your time, breath, energy, sanity, peace of mind and, years of life, thinking that they will change for you!. What I realized about a lot of women, who have stayed in abusive relationships and, marriages for long periods of time, is that we reminisce about the good moments that you shared with that person, that lead you to them.

Many women, in abusive relationships, tend to hold on to those sweet, delicate moments that once were, in hopes that you can get back to those caring moments with that person again.

We keep ourselves as victim's to these people, remembering the good times and, revisiting the past, when the relationship made you feel so good and, needed by them. There is an old saying that says, "When a person shows you who they really are, believe it"! That is who they really are. If you are in a relationship, and your mate is cursing at you with foul language, physically hitting you, beating you, putting you down, causing you tears and, grief, mentally, emotionally and, physically, all of this is abuse, you need to get out of this relationship fast! And, never look back!. Love does not hurt you, harm you or your children and, make you cry, that is not God's unconditional love at all!.

If a person, man, woman, boy or girl, is treating you this way, in front of family, strangers or friends, this is who they are. They may have started out wining and, dining you, buying you gifts, taking you out, cooking for you, talking to you so, sweet and, gentle. I know, because the men that abused me physically, emotionally and, mentally they started out treating me so, sweetly this way also.

But, after a while, it all went South! For the winter! And, their true self! Started to come to light. A person doesn't just wake up out of nowhere and, suddenly start to mistreat a person. That demon was lurking! Deep within them, camouflaged and, hiding behind a hidden, smiley mask, all the time!. You have to watch out for those small, first signs, that something may not be right with this person as you think. When that person, female or male, starts to show you these red flags, it may be God showing you to exit! To the nearest door!. Don't even wish them well! Disconnect yourself from these broken souls and, move forward! To what God has for you. God would never send a person to us, that would treat us this way, no! These people are who we choose for ourselves and, they were not sent by God!.

These broken souls can take you down some roads where you don't want to be and, in some cases, you can even lose your life! To the rage that is hidden within them.

There are so many women, men and, young adolescents, who have lost their lives, at the hands of an abuser, whether it be a boyfriend, girlfriend, spouse, relative or even parents. Abuse can happen even by the very, closest people that you loved and, trusted, not believing that they would ever harm or hurt you. If you have children, please have a talk with them early on about the different signs of abuse.

I would say, as early as they can understand what right and, wrong is, educate them about physical, emotional and, mental abuse from others and, what some of the signs are. One of my missions on this earth, is to help young girls and, women who are suffering or have been victim's as myself, of domestic violence and, sexual abuse. I pray that you, who are reading my book, take heed to the knowledge, messages and, information that I am sharing with you here from my spirit and, true heart. No one invested in me as a young child and, educated me about life. I was not prepared to know about relationships, friendships, marriage, abuse and, how to love myself. No one had talked to me about having self-love and, self-worth for myself, with healthy standards and, to aim high! For my future. Everything that I learned about life, I learned from the elders in the church, through my personal relationship with Christ and, myself studying the word of God, to learn about life outside of abuse.

My personal relationship that I have in Christ as his servant and, follower of him, is where I found my peace, safety, love and, directions in my life today. We need more programs within our communities, within our cities, organizations that addresses domestic violence and, sexual abuse. We need more mental health services that can help support our young and, older generation of people, who are suffering in silence. The old saying says, "It takes a village to raise the children" but, we need a village to help serve and, support everyone within our church walls and, community centers everywhere! Across the nation!. We as a people have to do more, than just stand at the pulpit and, give the same sermons, to the same people, that you preach to every Sunday. Jesus Christ preached from land to land with his Apostles and, followers by his side teaching as well. Jesus did not stay, sitting within the synagogues, delivering his messages of his father, no! He did not. Once Jesus taught his messages, that were given to him by his father, as a warning to the Pharisees and, Sadducees to turn! Back to the word of God!. Jesus and, his Apostles traveled on, spreading the good news! The word of God, to all! That would hear and, turn from their sins. We are the Church! The church is the people of God, not the building itself and it's many walls. Amen!

CHAPTER **6**

Spread Your Wings Like An Eagle- And Fly! High!..

AFTER SPENDING HALF of my life, off and, on for twenty five years, with my husband, arguing with him about his lifestyle, I knew that I had to make some changes. My husband was constantly causing arguments with my son's now that they were adults. I knew as my children had become adults in their late twenties and, thirties, that there were going to be some problems now. They now had a voice of their own and, after they had watched their mother get constantly mistreated by men in my life, I knew it all was coming to an end! Quickly!.

My youngest son had been run over by a vehicle and, left for dead at fourteen years old, right around the corner from my house, as I was on my knees praying one late evening. My husband was in prison, serving seven years, when this incident happened to my son and, I vowed to him that I would not wait seven years for him, not this time again, since we were not married yet.

I had met and, dated a couple of people during his seven years in prison and, even married a guy, who was raising his twelve year old son. By the first year of our marriage, I had rededicated my life back over to Christ and, God called me forward, to be a minister within my church home at that time. I was done with living my life, outside of the will of God for good!. My then husband was great in every area of our marriage, but he too was sleeping with other women, outside of our marriage. He moved in with me, with his son, with my children and, we became a beautiful loving family I thought. He had never done any drugs, we both didn't drink, he didn't hang out in the streets or with his buddies and, he didn't curse or abuse me in any type of way.

We both were the same age, back then, and, we got along well, and our children too. He drove tanker trucks for a living and, he paid the rent and, every bill in the house himself, as I too went to work. He would tell me, to keep the money that I made, for the children's needs and, myself and, it blew! My mind!. I was now in college, moving forward to be an mental health and substance abuse counselor. He brought me flowers, chocolate candy and, cards for no reason at all and, he kept the car full of gas, with my favorite fruit drinks, in a small ice cooler that he put in the car for me to go to work. That was something that no man had ever done for me in my entire life!. He took me around his parents, family and, his closest friends and, I thought, finally, I had a real man, sent to me by God!. Wrong! Again! Wow!.

Behind all of those great qualities and, gentlemen type behavior towards me, his wife, he was still sleeping with the mother of his nine year old daughter behind my back. I loved him because he had a strong sense of family values and, he always made me first over his family and, friends. But, behind all of the great qualities that he had, he also had a fake! Mask on and, he had a silent, traumatic, childhood past that was lurking to come forth! Inside of him too. He was also a broken man inside! With invisible wounds, just like the rest of us were.

Once I found out about his affairs it was all over between us within a year of marriage and, he moved out with his son. I divorced him two years later and, I never saw him again, but his son stayed in contact with me, and my children for many years. Why do these types of men play with the hearts of women, who want to be in a monogamous, faithful relationship with only them I had asked God? And, myself. They know coming in the door, that they are not going to settle down with one woman. So, why continue to lie, manipulate, gaslight women and, make us believe that they are ready for love and, commitment, when they are not?. These types of men have no self control over their bodies and, have no personal relationship with Christ either. Without that true spirit of God within you, to guide your ways and, your thoughts, you cannot defeat those demonic forces over your life, without God being head of your life and, your family. You can't win!. If you are a man and, you are not ready to settle down, with one woman by your side, don't marry or have children with these innocent women. Why don't they just stay out there with the women who are just like them! And, leave! These (Us) decent women alone! Leave the women alone, who are looking to settle down, with one man, in hopes of a committed marriage. They should go and, be with the men or women who are just like them!. Out of all the men that I had dated throughout my life and, two, broken marriages now, all of them had suffered with some form of sexual, physical abuse, and, childhood trauma, from their parents and, other peers in their lives. These cycles and, patterns of traumatic abuse, within a family generation is real!. Let me continue on with my story here.

My youngest child, as I said, had nearly lost his life, as a victim of hit and, run at fourteen years young. He laid on life support, his body broken up and, the skin was torn from his face, arms, chest and, legs from being thrown ten feet, up the street from the impact of the car that left the scene and, was never found. Through my prayers, the prayers of the saints of God and, the community of neighbors, God spared my son's life, after almost a year of physical therapy. We prayed my son off of life support, within seven days, later, from being put on the machine to breathe. That's God's! Loving power! Amen!. He heard the saints of God, our prayers, crying out to him! And, God answered our prayers, on my child's behalf. He lives!.

Then by the age of fifteen, my same son was targeted by gangs, twice on two, separate occasions and, shot for not joining their gang. My son was shot once in the arm, which had to be rebuilt with pipes and, bolts for him to be able to use again. Then, six months later, my son was shot again in his ankle, targeted a second time, by the same gangs, who wanted him to join their gang, as he was walking by my sister's and, mother's house, visiting them that day. The gang members were determined to take my son's life, for not joining their gang. But, God spared my child's life, because he had a praying mother! Who was sold out to Christ! Living a full! Life! Dedicated and, obedient unto the word of God!.

At thirty, one years young today, despite some mental delays, from the brain injury that my son sustained, from being run over by the car that hit him, my son still lives! Today and, he is doing well. All! Praise! Be unto God!. As you can see, even my children have faced multiple challenges in their life, set out by the enemy to destroy them, but God said no! Each time. My daughter had a cancerous tumor removed, just in time from one of her lungs, at the age of twenty four. I prayed and, prayed over my daughter, my child's life to be healed by God, along with the saints of God too. My baby was terrified and, so was I at times, but I continued to trust the Lord and, my daughter is now thirty, two years old today and, cancer free!. Prayer does change things, if you are walking upright, in the word of God and, you believe! Amen!. Some things God will heal or change for us and, some things we will have to suffer and, lose, even in our faith. But, that doesn't mean that God doesn't love us or that he doesn't hear our prayers, we must accept the good and, bad things that will happen to us in our lives, sometimes.

We have no idea how life will hit us here on this earth, or why things happen the way that they do, but there will be, trying circumstances that will come. All I know and, trust is that if we lean on Jesus Christ and, his will for our lives, God will give us the strength to endure and, move forward. Amen!

God has always been the head of my life, from a twelve year old, curious girl, who was filled with the Holy Spirit back then. I don't know where I would be in my life or mentally today, if I allowed my circumstances to overcome my faith in God, to see me through all that I suffered. Don't you tell me that prayer doesn't change things, because in many of our circumstances that we face, prayer does help to change things for our good. Myself and, my children's life is a living testimony! Of the power! Of prayer and, that God will deliver, heal and, come to your rescue, in your time of need. God will call out to us, in our times of need and, say, Where Art Thou!? To our spirit. We have to trust the process, my dear readers here.

God says, in the scriptures it reads in, Psalm Ch. 18 Vs. 35-36 it reads, Thou hast also given me the shield of thy salvation: and thy right hand hath Holden me up, and thy gentleness hath made me great. V. 36 Thou hast enlarged my steps under me, that my feet did not slip. Amen!. God loves each and, everyone of us, God will keep you in your times of need and, give us the ability to endure our worst and, most painful! Moments in life. He did it for me and, God will be there for you as well.

After my son's vicious, three attacks on his life, I decided to move to a more expensive and, gated community in the Gold Coast and, River North Side of Chicago. I prayed for God to lead me in a new direction, to keep and, protect my son from constantly being targeted by gangs, on the Southside and, Southeast side of Chicago, where these particular areas are the most violent areas in the city to live in. My children have lost dozens of friends and, people they knew, through the senseless, gun violence that is constantly taking lives here in our city.

The change of community and, environment has worked out well, for me and, my son. We have adjusted very quickly to the busy, downtown, Chicago lifestyle and, we don't hear all of the police sirens, ambulances and, fire truck sirens, racing up and, down the streets, all day and, night, like when we were living in those drug infested, gang infested and, crime ridden communities most of our lives. Finally in my thirties, I had worked my way up the ladder, getting my Associates Degree in Behavior Science, through Olive Harvey College Bridge Program in the 90tys, transferring over to Kennedy King College on the Southside of the Englewood community. From there I received my Bachelor's Degree in Applied Behavioral Science, continuing in the counseling field at National Louis University, in the downtown Chicago campus University. Having these college degrees has helped me to get employment at many top hospitals and, agencies working with mental health and, substance abuse patients and, clients for twenty, six years now. I am currently finishing my Masters degree, as a clinical counselor right now, at The Chicago Professional School of Psychology praise God! That I am almost done with.

My life, at fifty, one years young now, I decided to advance, so that I can prepare for my latter years ahead. Through everything that I have suffered, experienced and, gone through, I never lost my faith in God and, I never stopped believing in myself. I knew that my past life does not define who God made molded and, created me to be today.

I made my father so proud of me, he got to see me walk across the stage twice, before I led him to Christ and, he closed his eyes to glory. My father was rapidly dying from fourth stage, lung cancer when he passed away and, he still came to my first and, second graduation. I remembered him walking on a cane and, he was in so much pain, to see his big baby, walk proudly, across that stage, receiving my Bachelor's Degree, before he passed away, months later, I will never forget those precious moments that me and, my children spent, for many years, barbecuing and, spending our time with my daddy.

Despite all the bad things that he did to my mother and, family, I understood his fight inside and, pains that he suffered with, from his upbringing and, silent trauma that he hide within himself too. He did have some great moments with my mother, throughout their years together and, my father protected her, me and, my siblings as best he could. I loved him unconditionally, because he was that strong, intelligent, powerful, brave, unfearing, handsome, smart and, loving dad to me. I was and, still am to this day, of him being gone, a daddy's girl!.

My father told me multiple times how much he loved me and, he thanked me for moving in with him at my grandma's house, and, for caring for him, the last year of his life. I truly miss him dearly and, I know that I will see him again in heaven one-day. God's word says, to be absent from the body is to be present with the Lord!. What an beautiful! And, amazing! Place, for all of us true, righteous, saints of God to be, when we leave this old body, to live for eternity! With the Lord one-day soon. Amen!

Even though I had done well with my life, moving up step by step, my husband, he just could not, would not adjust to living a peaceful, comfortable new life, in our mixed community, and, our building of luxury, living. We had gotten back together years later, after my first divorce, when he was serving seven years in prison. When I moved in with my father, he was coming to visit me regularly at my father's house, spending a lot of time with us. He had been writing letters to my grandmother's house, during his seven years he spent in prison, when I had gotten married. I eventually responded to the letters, surprisingly, that my uncle had been putting away, who lived in the house with my father. This is how I got back with my husband, during those months that my father was dying right before my eyes. My husband was the only person who was there with me, as my father was passing away and, supporting me. My sister refused to come over with her children to see my father, out of her anger from those abusive years, when my father was with my mother.

Mind you that was over twenty five years ago, but, my sister never had a real love for our father or forgave him. Neither did my three brothers as well. They never fully forgave our father from the past and, my second, oldest brother, only came once, from a three, hour car ride, to see my father, when he was passing away. My oldest brother called, but he never came to see my father at all. I quit my job and, me and, my youngest son, moved into my father's house to take care of him. Two other brothers of my father lived there in the house with my father too and, one of my father's brothers there, was horrible! Towards me, while I was living there, caring for my fathers needs.

I was under constant attacks by some of my father's relative's, who were just as evil as evil could be, towards me, as I was trying to take my father to his Radiation and, Chemotherapy treatments, four days a week. I was picking up his medications, cooking breakfast, lunch and, dinner for us, washing his clothes and, buying his food for us to eat. I did it all alone with the unconditional love of God in my spirit and, heart with only my son, my husband and, God by my side.

When my father died, I paid for my father's memorial service, and, my Bishop at the time, eulogized my father's memorial service, along with some of the Ministers and, other parishioners of our church for free. After the cremation, I was spiritually, emotionally and, mentally dead! Inside and, I just wanted to get as fast! Away from that demonic house, where my father lived. There was no love in that house at all! And, I prayed over me, my son and, father several times a day, to withstand the evilness that was within the people in that house!. I remembered the main brother that was calling himself running the house, told my father one-day, that he hoped he died, without any remorse. His two brothers that lived there, were actually mocking the fact that my father was dying. My father paid all the bills in that house and, did all the repairs to the old, badly worn house of my grandmothers. My father did all the repairs when some of his sisters and, brothers needed help on their cars and, home for years. At the memorial service, not one of them would get up and, say one kind word about my father, but I spoke for my family on his behalf.

I still pray for my father's relative's to this day and, I walked away from that house and, family forgiving them all, as Christ would want me to do. I brought the light of God within me, when I moved into that house and, when my father passed away, when I left that house, trust and, know, that the light that I brought within me, over there, left too!. Okay, back to the story.

My husband, as I said, we had moved to the Gold Coast community in downtown Chicago, after my father passed away and as usual, my husband was soon behaving back to his old, negative patterns, as before and, I knew it wasn't going to end well this last and, final time between us.

He loved to hang around toxic, negative people and, places that were just like him. He did not like the fact that I had surrendered my life over to Christ during his prison times and, also that I had advanced in my education and, career.

God showed me that he had a silent envy and, jealousy against me, I saw it, felt it and, others saw it too. When I gave him a ticket to come to my graduation at the McCormick center, I will never forget what he said to me. He told me, "I don't want to go, because that should be me walking across the stage". My father, who was dying from fourth stage lung cancer and, he limped, side by side with me, walking that huge, long corridor, to the stadium, for us graduates. And, here was my husband healthy and he had money to take a bus to my graduation or Uber ride to my graduation, to see me get my Bachelor's Degree. He refused to come, because he felt humiliated, because it was not him!. After I had spent twenty, five years of my life, supporting him, all of his prison terms and, visiting him in and, out of rehabs, that he would sign himself out of, each time he went in. All the years of his cheating, committing adultery, his verbal and, mental abuse, on my special day, he made it about himself, his failure to do something with his life, other than chasing loose women, drugs and, alcohol, all of his fifty, six year old life. His envy, jealousy and, pride would not allow him to come support his loyal wife, on another proud accomplishment that I worked hard to accomplish, for my future ahead with him.

The same man, who traveled on greyhound buses, with his friends to different events out of state, he rode the bus to meet up with his buddies and, women friends that he hung out with and, to their dinner parties and, their functions. But, he refused selfishly and, with a Covert narcissistic behavior and, attitude all about himself, on the day of my graduation with my mother, father, sister and, my children present at my side. That hurt me in more ways than one. He did attend my graduation dinner, party that my uncle and, his wife had for me, at their small church with my family and, friends being present, from my job that I was working at. After that day, I never looked at him the same way again.

My husband didn't really support anything positive that I did, to support us all. Just like how my mother didn't have a voice with my father, I didn't have any voice with my husband either. He was a one man show and, my husband had an affair the first month that we said, I do, so, he never had any intentions on committing to me or God in this marriage from day one.

I realized that I should have left him many years ago and, I never should have married him, because he was never, mentally, emotionally and, spiritually stable within. I was always last, to his friends, his women and, the streets. My husband did not like my submission to God, he did not want to go to church with me or do anything that had anything to do with God and, that was scary! To witness a person, up front, denounce God!.

Unfortunately there will be a lot of people just like my husband, who have refused God and, seek the help that they need psychologically. Unfortunately, many of them, like my husband, will sadly die in that destructive condition and, never see heaven, when the Lord returns. We also have to understand that it is their choice to die or live their lives however they choose to live it and, in most cases there is nothing humanly possible that we can do about it. We have to give them over to God and, hope that they are willing to change their lives for themselves one-day.

My former Bishop, who ordained me as a minister many years ago, told me once, that the people who refuse to surrender their life over to Christ and, turn from their wicked ways, that they have a right to go to hell! Or heaven! That is their own personal choice. Ouch! How powerful! Of a statement that was, but so, true.

Have you ever done everything in your power to help to save someone that you loved, from their destructive lifestyle, that was harming them and, destroying you all at the same time?. I know many of you reading this book have experienced this with a loved one that you fought tooth! And, nail! To help them. But, in the end, the one that winded up with the most wounds and, battle scars is you!.

Believe me from my years of trying to help people to save themselves, you will burn! Completely out! Trying, pleading and, constantly talking to them over and, over again, until you have a stroke! Or a heart attack! Fighting them. You will be dead and, they will still be doing the same thing, when you yourself are kicking daisies! Up! From your grave.

It's just not worth your sanity, your health and, your peace of mind, to keep battling and, fighting for people that do not! Want to be saved! Or change!. We all have to come to a point in our lives, where we have to give these broken and, tormented souls over to Christ, dust your feets at the door and, move! On! Let Them go! For you!.

If they crash! And burn! There is nothing that you could have done more to help them, they chose their own paths and, we have to get out of the way! And, let God deal with them, in his own will. It says in the scriptures in Matthew Ch. 10 Vs. 12 Th 14 it reads, [12] As you enter the home, give it your greeting. [13] If the home is deserving, let your peace rest on it; if it is not, let your peace return to you. [14] If anyone will not welcome you or listen to your words, leave that home or town and shake the dust off your feet. Amen! You have to let them go! Save yourself!.

We hold on to broken people, many of us for too long! Thinking that we can heal them and, fix them and, we do not have that kind of power of God to fix anyone but ourselves with God's power!. The person that you will lose is yourself! Like I did. Move forward, to the best! That God has designed for just you.

We have to upgrade our thinking about ourselves and, know that we deserve better. It is time that we start learning how to love ourselves enough, to know that you (We) are worthy to be treated and, respected by people, that will be loyal and, have unconditional love for you. We have to refuse to allow any person to physically, emotionally and, mentally abuse us. Let go! And, wait on the Lord and, watch God bring his best! For you (Us) in his timing and, will. After all you (We) are worth it!. Amen! Let me continue with the story.

The Camel that broke the straws back, with my husband, and, I finally said enough, was his violent behavior, adultery and, disrespect towards me and, my youngest son. His behavior had gotten out of human control for me and, my mental, emotional and, physical health was rapidly deteriorating!. I was slaving, on the job working twelve hours on the night shifts, four days a week and, caring for our puppy, "Miracle" who was our Emotional Support Dog and, my mentally challenged son.

I had been battling my sister, who had total control over my mother at this time too. I had been told about some things going on, with my mother's care, by my mother and, my sister's oldest daughter. So, I intervened at my mother's request and, her daughter's request to do so. I had taken my mother from my sister and left my mother at my daughter's apartment, while I went to work that night. They sent someone to my daughter's apartment and took my mother without my daughter's knowledge a week later unfortunately.

After that everyone turned on me and, made me out to be the "Villain" in the end. I was put in a situation to remove my mother from their house, to take care of her needs and, then I was Black Balled! By them all, as if they never told me, about all the bad things that were taking place with my sister and, my sister's last child's father, who lived with her too. These are the same family members that I took in my home, for years, everywhere I went. I spent money on them, bought for them and, gave money to them for years and, I never turned my back on any of them, not once, in their time of need.

As of today, I have not seen any of them, not even my dear, sweet mother, who has been conditioned and, has no voice still, in four years, by my own, sisters' enforcement, against my will. This is typically what happens when you intervene and, try to help family or friends with their problems. In the end, most times, these same people will turn on you, betray you and, your heart. It hurts you to your very core inside, when you know that you have done nothing wrong and, that your intentions were pure. But, today, I have given the situation over to God, these last four years and, I continue to pray over my family, that we come to terms about it all and, love one another as we should, as family. Another tactic of the enemy, to divide, Kill, steal and, destroy! Families and, we fall for the same manipulative tricks, against each other every time. My Lord!

I pray for God's protection over them and, for God to bring peace in his timing and, will over the healing of my family. I trust and, I believe in God's will, that this too shall pass! There is hope ahead. In the scriptures it says in, Proverbs Ch. 3 Vs. 5 Th 6 it reads, [5] Trust in the Lord with all thine heart; and lean not unto thine own understanding.[6] In all thy ways acknowledge him, and he shall direct thy paths. Amen!

I know many of you, yourselves have witnessed this same type of demonic forces of division within your own family and, it's so hard at times, to walk away from the people that you love. It's not easy to let go, but when it gets to the point where you are giving more than you are receiving, it may be time for you to pull back and, regroup in your prayers with God, for the right decision and, choices that you need to make, concerning the matter. In my battles, against my sister, her daughter and, my mother and, other family members, they are now in the care of the Lord! I am done here. I also had to accept the reality about my husband and, his behavior, that he was doing his best, to pull me backwards, from the person that God changed me from being. We lived in a no smoking, community building, with about two hundred and, fifty units of different ethnicities of people. Mainly, White, Palestinians, Jewish and, some Black people, it was a great community, where we lived and, peaceful. We had a swimming pool, rooftop patio overlooking the John Hancock building. We had a full, state of the art, exercise facility, a dog park in the building, four party rooms, with pool tables and, seventy, five inch televisions, in all of the party rooms to enjoy.

This was the first time in my life that I was living the life that I had dreamed about with my son, we even had a coffee shop in our first floor lobby. God had upgraded me tremendously, through all the suffering that I had endured, from my mother's womb, till now. Instead of my husband celebrating with me, the blessings of the Lord, upgrading us, in a safe and, beautiful community, he did everything in his power to set us backwards!.

My husband would smoke cigarettes throughout the apartment

when I wasn't home and, he would go into the exit hallways to smoke and, the tenants were reporting me constantly to the managers, who had an office right in our lobby. I ended up with two lease warnings, because of my husband's behavior and, breaking the lease rules.

Not to forget me and, my son were asthmatics and, he would not even stop smoking in the house, for the safety of our lungs, while I was at work. He would put food on the stove at night drunk, once he came in and, nearly burned! The kitchen down, falling asleep on the couch a few times.

Me and, my son would jump up from our bed, hearing the fire detectors, go off in our kitchen and, we would have to open the windows, to let the smoke out of the house. No matter how many times that I talked to my husband in heated arguments, yelling and, screaming at eachother, he would not stop what he was doing, to harm me and, jeopardize our place to stay. This horrible behavior from him went on for the complete two and, a half years that I had moved us downtown, for a new way of living for us all.

I had him removed from our place, by calling his parole office, to remove him. He was gone for about two months and, he had to live in a shelter, because all of his so- called buddies and, the women that he slept with, wouldn't even give him a pillow! To lay his head in their house. (No surprise right?). Eventually, after three months, I allowed him to come back, to work things out, as he said he wanted to do. But, the behavior pattern never changed and, he confessed to me that he had fathered a baby, with a young, twenty something year old girl, who had other children. I knew it in my spirit, that he was out there living in adultery, because a woman's intuition is never wrong, before I found out the truth.

I went through his cell phone when he came in drunk, one late night and, I found out that it was four women that he had been dealing with in total, during the two years that we lived downtown. I read all of the messages from each woman and, that street! Hood! Side of me came out for only a moment and, I texted all the mistresses, letting them all know who I was to him and, that they could permanently!

Have him! Because I was done! And, that I would pray for them, for intervening in a marriage. My husband was such a Covert! Narcissist! He actually thought that I was going to accept this child, born into our marriage and, help him to raise this child, with his mistress, who was younger than my twenty, seven years old baby son, who lived with us. My husband was fifty, four years old, I believe when I found out about the child. He only confessed about the child to me, because I had found out about all the women and, the evidence in his phone that night.

He wanted me to help him to raise this child, with his mistresses. Can you believe this? What arrogance! Right?. He had no shame or remorse for what he had done to destroy my heart and, our marriage.

Narcissists are known to do whatever they have to, to get what they want and, they have no remorse or conscience for hurting and, harming good people. As of today, my prayer is not for any harm to be brought upon my husband no, I have forgiven him within my spirit today. I pray for his soul, that he surrenders his life over to Christ, walks upright in God's commandments and, turns from his sins before he breathes no more.

But, FINALLY! I was done! And, God said to my spirit, my child, I am proud of you, for your strong faith and, endurance to carry so much pain and, still trust me. God spoke to my heart, and, he said to my spirit, that those tests were over! And, for me to give all of my burdens over to him and, I did. Once I heard this is my spirit, I felt those years of burdens fall off of me! And, I was now free!. I had to let them all go! For my peace of mind and, for my health's sake too, that was deteriorating. I had stopped taking care of myself and, in my depression and, constant fight! Or flight! Mode with my husband. My weight had shot up to two, hundred and, seventy seven pounds, after we got back together. My husband and, his sinful and, destructive behavior was killing! Me and, It was time for me to put this demon in my life to rest!. I realized that I was definitely sleeping with the enemy!.

In 2022, I moved out of our place, downtown with my son, to another, beautiful, gated community, up north, by Montrose Beach and, my husband moved to another shelter, before moving to another city, four hours away from Chicago. It's amazing to me, that out of all the women that he was dealing with, all of the buddies that he partied day and, night with and, he had spent his money with these women and, buddies, from the odd jobs that he worked. Not one! Of them gave him a place to stay with them, after I had left him and, moved on with my son, without him, this time for good!. How about that?. He had to stay in shelters and, recovery homes, for men who were freshly out of prison and, were recovering addicts. A friend that he knew, allowed him to come out of the city, with him, until he was able to get a job and, his own place out there. Plus, he now had a child that he had to send money to the mother, to help with, since she also had other children. Come to find out, the young girl's life was just as messed up! As his life was, his daughter's mother. He found comfort in women and, men that were just as destructive and, toxic as his lifestyle was. My change, that I had made, my new walk in Christ, while he was going in and, out of prison, he could not accept. I wanted better! For myself and, my family and, I no longer was this lost, damaged and, broken girl that he had fell in love with twenty, six years ago. I no longer felt low self-esteem about who I now was and, I was now educating myself, with my third college degree, when he got out, that last time. I now had a voice and, I wanted no parts of the broken and, damaged lifestyle that I lived, for years fighting and, arguing with him, about his destructive lifestyle, I wanted out!. That was no longer my lifestyle anymore. But, he did not want that type of change, so, he did everything that he could to pull me backwards and, to tare! Me down!.

I told him the day that I was moving out, that me and, him were done! And, the marriage was over! And I wished him well. Twenty, five years of pain and, betrayal that I suffered from my husband was now over!. Once me and, my son had moved into our new place, it took about two weeks for me to mentally and, physically relax, before we unpacked the boxes and, I started to feel like our new place was home!. The big! Bad! Witch! In my life was now dead! To God! I give! All the praise!. I had survived losing our place to live three times, due to health issues, when I left my husband, I had to walk away from two jobs, working in the hospital, due to discrimination and, I lost two jobs, due to sickness. My life didn't just get better and, stay better, because I left my husband, the enemy continued to attack my health, mental and, my income once I left my husband and, my family were gone from me. But, I never gave! Up! I got back up! And, began the work each time over again, in a new and, better place to live and, I landed, better jobs than the jobs that I had lost, before that one. Each place that I got, was in a better, gated community, than the one, that I had moved from, three times in a two year period.

Once I finally got our house together, I PRAISED! God! For a new, fresh! Start to life and, I cried, cried and, cried! Probably for the entire month each time that I moved into a new place with joy! The three times that I had to move, after leaving my husband. God had removed every person and, all of the distractions out of my life now, that had been crippling! Me for over thirty years. I will be divorcing my husband eventually, but right now, my focus is on my mental, emotional, physical and, spiritual healings. Right now, I am allowing God to direct my path, towards my next journeys ahead that God has for me. I have been in isolation, by God, for two years now, since I left my husband September 27th of 2022 and, it feels good'T! With a capital "T", I feel my strength and, my health improving.

Due to my husband, his multiple affairs within our marriage, in adultery, according to scripture, I have the legal right, biblically to divorce him and, be set free! The scripture reads in Matthew Ch. 19 Vs. 9 it reads, And I say unto you, Whosoever shall put away his wife, except it be for fornication, and shall marry another, committeth adultery: and whoso marrieth her which is put away doth commit adultery. Amen! So, if your spouse is found to have committed adultery within the marriage, you, according to God's scripture, you are allowed to divorce them and, move on with your life.

It is troubling when a man or woman will throw away and, lose their family, for another person, who is not worth losing your family. I have witnessed throughout my life men, women, Pastors and,

Bishops, having affairs behind their spouses back and, them losing their wife or husband in the end. Like my dear, sweet, friend of mine, once said to me, "One false move! Can cost you everything!".

A few minutes of pleasure has a price for you to pay, when it's all said and, done, the enemy will come to collect! And, you will lose!. If you have a great partner in your life, support them, appreciate them and, keep them close to your heart. Because, God may not bless you with another partner like the one that you had again. To lose a great man or woman in your life, is like looking for a needle in a haystack! Today. it's just not worth it, trust my word it's not, hurting and, betraying the one that you are supposed to love unconditionally. There is no guarantee that your partner will forgive you, for your wrongs and, take you back, so don't take a gamble on that, because you just might strike! Out!.

Even though I had to leave my husband after twenty- five years off and, on with him, I prayed for many, many years before the throne of God for my husband's soul!. Even before we married, I prayed for him constantly, throughout those hard and, rough years, dealing with all of his abuse and, addictions that he suffered with. It was days when I sat him down, when he was sober to pray with me to God and, sometimes he would. I prayed throughout our marriage, because I did not want to walk away from my marriage, for a second time, when I was forced to divorce my first husband for adultery. I prayed for my husband and, his soul, more than I prayed for my own life!.

That's that part of unconditional love, when you pray for another person's soul, more than you do for your own. I prayed for my husband, the same way with intensity, that I prayed for my mother and, my three children, whom I gave birth to from my womb. That's how much and, how badly I wanted my husband's soul to be free! From the darkness that he loved so much and, for him to walk beside me in the light of Jesus Christ in heaven. But, he did not want it for himself.

People say to me, why him? You didn't have any children with him, so, why did you stay in that relationship with him for so long, when You could have easily walked away?. I stood all of those years with this one man, because I had UNCONDITIONAL Love for him! And, I wanted to fight for him, the twenty, five years and, our marriage. But, as I wrote earlier, we tend to cling and, attach ourselves to people who have the same type of familiar spirit as you. I met my husband when I had just ran away from a almost five year, brutally, physically, abusive relationship with my children's father. Not to forget that I had been around nothing but broken, tormented, dark souls, of family, and, friends all of my natural born life.

Even though I surrendered my life back over to Christ, way before we got back together, I still had a desire and, love deep within me to be with him, because we had twenty, five years of history together. I was saved, I had a strong relationship with Christ and, I had educated myself to aim higher for me and, my children's future, during his incarcerated years, away from us. But, I still wrestled with some sickness within me, that was still fighting the spirit of God, that was within me, to let these demonic and, toxic people go!. I didn't want to leave the very people that I loved behind, I wanted them to taste the goodness of God's love and, healings within me and, I felt like I was the closest thing to God that they ever knew!. I was fighting against God's warnings unto me, with a thorn! In my side and, I didn't want to leave my family or husband behind. I allowed all of them, for many years, to mistreat me and, betray me, over and, over again.

I felt guilty in some strange way, that I grew, matured and, defeated all the odds that were stacked against me by society. A poor, impoverished, Black girl, who came from an abusive and, unloving family. A dropout from highschool, a teenage mother, who was raised in the heart of one of the worst parts of Chicago, which was the Englewood community at that time, in the 80s and, 90s.

I rose up! Out of that stigma! In my life and, I asked God to make me over! And, he did!. God saved my soul from hell, I am a college graduate, at fifty, one years young, about to graduate with my third college degree, my Masters degree. Me and, my son are living in the downtown area of Chicago's meg mile, from where I was raised in the gang infested, high murder and, crime ridden communities of Englewood, Southwest and, Southeast side of Chicago with my three children and, we survived! It all praise! God!. We live!

If you want to change your life, overcome your past traumas and, setbacks in your life, if you want it and, you put God first in your life it can! Be done!. I am a walking testimony and, proof! That it can be done!. Amen!

But, as I said before, you can pray for a person until you are blue! In the face. If they are not praying to God for change for themselves, and, if they don't desire their own change, there is absolutely nothing! That you can do to help them!. They have to do the work for themselves!.

God put on my heart, cut! The umbilical cord! From these people, you cannot continue to allow people to eat all of the healthy fruits off of your tree, let it be, Finished!. I still love my husband even today and, I will always have him in my prayers that he surrenders his life over to Christ before he closes his eyes. I am more concerned about his soul being set free! Than for us to get back together again. Unless my husband turns from his sinful ways and, he surrenders his life to Christ, fully, God cannot heal nor forgive him of his sins, and his soul will remain in the hands of the enemy. My prayer is for my husband to be delivered in Christ, at his own will, to do so.

I have never in my life had this much peace and, joy within me, since God removed all of the toxic, wicked and, Covert narcissist people, out of me and, my children's life today. God has put me in isolation away from everyone, for almost three years now, as I said earlier. I sit with God alone, talking to him, praying daily, studying the scriptures, worshiping in song and, prayer. I am working on myself inside and, out for my healing, self-care and, self-love. It feels good'T! With a capital "T" On me today, Hello! Somebody!. You can have it for yourself too, if you desire it bad enough. Amen! God is waiting for us to call out to him in our prayers, so that he can call out to us and, ask us, Where Art Thou!?. Amen!

I am finding my place in life, in my fifties, how about that!?. It is a strange new world for me now and, it is a little scary, starting all over again at my age I won't lie. God is remodeling and, shaping me right now, I am just going through his process, like squeezing oil from an olive, in the grinder or presser. Once I realized my worth and, value today, I have learned to love me, for who I am and, to always put myself first over others. I will no longer allow any person to treat me as if I am an option! and, not a priority! Not today I won't. I am a Black woman, an aire to King! Jesus Christ in heaven! And, my name is written in the book of life!.

I am somebody, my voice matters in this world and, I deserve to be loved unconditionally, treated with respect and, loyalty by people, as I pour it back into others as well. I am a daughter, a mother, a grandmother, a sister, a niece, a cousin, an auntie, a friend, an associate, an educator. I am a servant! To God's children, a counselor, a partner, a nurturer, a lover of God's love to share, a follower of Christ, a worshiper to God and, a leader!. I birth three, human lives from within my womb and, I am a minister! Of the word of God!. This is who I am! Through Christ who strengthens me!, Aka- "Pooky" the nickname that my parents gave me from birth.

CHAPTER 7

Yea, Though I Walk Through The Valley Of The Shadow Of Death, I Will Fear No Evil!:

ISAIAH CH. 43 Vs.18 Th19 it reads, ¹⁸ Remember ye not the former things, neither consider the things of old.¹⁹ Behold, I will do a new thing; now it shall spring forth; shall ye not know it? I will even make a way in the wilderness, and rivers in the desert. Amen!

Sometimes you may have to walk through this life alone, and, trust the Lord moving forward. People will be with you, as long as things are going smoothly, I have learned this the hard way, through my struggles. Once things started going downhill with my relationships, job, income and, health, everyone from the beginning with me is now gone!. My phone ain't ringing with them calling to check on me anymore. As soon as I buckled down and, I began to share my walk with Christ with them and, all the new changes that I was making for my peace and, spirit, folks really lost my number!. Even the chirps! Of the birds! Went away!.

People were not celebrating with me, when I decided to get out of the losing team! And, I started doing something different with my life. They were not happy for me, some of you have been there in your own lives. When you became happy, better, and, started upgrading your life, people became envious, and, jealous of you and, their true colors, started to come out!. I call people like that silent assassin's! In disguise!. Watch those within your circle, study them and, pray to God about them for clarity, before you make people worthy enough to call a friend.

When I was sitting on the phone in depression with them, wasting time, talking about our problems in our relationship with men, family problems, job problems and, gossipping away, I got three to four calls a day, seven days a week from folks!. The minute that I was know longer entertaining the gossip, and, depressing, old stuff of the past, people didn't want to hang on the phone with me anymore.

I wanted to bring up God in our conversations, talk about his love, how he has changed me and, I wanted to talk about new beginnings of life. And, people dropped! Me like a hot! Skillet! And, that was the end of our conversations. They didn't want to hear about my positive changes, or my new outlook on life. They wanted to stay in that toxic! Negative patterns and, cycles of a broken spirit. I know longer wanted to be a part of that dark crowd anymore and, they wanted to stay stuck in the past! So, I had to let them go! To be whom God had called me out to be, in the light with him.

It's so funny to me today, because God had to open my eyes, for me to see that they were never friends to me anyway, because true! friendship! Will be with you until the end!. So, I realized that I didn't have any friends, like I thought, who were truly by my side. Thank you Lord! For showing me the kind of people that I had in my life and, most importantly, thank you! Lord! For removing them for me. I lost years and, years! Of dead weight! From others, who should not have been on my boat anyway. After all, it worked out for my good! And I can dig that today.

When people abandon you in your time of need and, the phone calls stop coming in, don't miss them! Because they were never truly for you anyway! That's why they bailed out on you! So, easily in your time of need. You should be proud that they are gone, so that God can usher in the right people that he has to connect with you, on your new journeys ahead!. Get excited! Because it's time for the new!.

When you reinvent yourself, in most cases, you will have to start all over from scratch as I am right now, as I write this book to help educate you and, to encourage you along the way. Keep moving! Forward! And, Don't you dare! Look back or go back! To those doors that God closed!. Praise God!.

We can't keep looking backwards, at the things that shouldn't have been in our lives anyway. Those situations that we went through, some, were lessons that we had to learn, whether they were good, bad, or ugly we had to go through those processes anyway. We don't know and, may never get the answers from God as to why we had to suffer and, lose so much along the way. I don't know myself and, all I know is that God is God and, he does not have to tell us why he allows things to happen in our lives the way it does. Maybe once we make it to heaven, the ones of us who are going to be raptured up! Maybe we will find it all out, once we arrive in the presence of the Lord on that good day.

As of today, I am fifty, one years young, separated from my spouse, taking care of my son, myself and, our beloved dog. I still have some things that I am struggling with right now, but through it all, I will not allow the enemy to discourage me and, stop me from getting to the place in my life that God has for me! My three beautiful children and, my adorable, eleven grandchildren too. I could easily use all of these horrible things that have happened to me, from the time I was in my mother's womb until now, to give up. I could give the enemy my power and, roll over and, die! But I won't!.

I could use all of these situations to go back into the world and, live within the sins of this world, turning my back completely on my faith and, belief in Christ, but I will not!.

That is what the enemy wants us to do, when the problems of this world hits us. His job, the enemy, is to take away as many lives as he can, before the Lord returns and, to divide the family unit. The scripture says, in John Ch. 10 Vs.10 it reads, [10] The thief cometh not, but for to steal, and to kill, and to destroy: I am come that they might have life, and that they might have it more abundantly. Amen!

Some of my readers, you may have had parents or a parent murdered, or killed in an accident and, loved ones, who passed away from sudden health issues. You may have had children or a child killed, who passed away in an accident or taken away from you without understanding. You may have lost grandparents and, other loved ones, who were close and, dear to your heart as well. You may have lost close friends, who you grew up with, you talked to them all the time and, you hung out with them and, now they are now gone. Many of you may even be angry, bitter and, have become weary in your faith in God, because you don't understand why your loved one was taken away from you so soon.

As I said, we don't have the answers, as to why things happen the way that they do, but life's challenges will happen to us all, good or bad people. None of us are exempt from life's pain, hurt, betrayal, discouragement, death, losses, health issues and, those weary days that will come. But, I can assure you according to the scriptures, that God does not want any of us to perish, but for us who believe in him, to have everlasting life with him in heaven. it says, in John Ch. 3 Vs. 16-17 it reads, [16] For God so loved the world, that he gave his only begotten Son, that whosoever believeth in him should not perish, but have everlasting life.[17] For God sent not his Son into the world to condemn the world; but that the world through him might be saved. Amen! God wants us all to be with him in eternity one-day.

In our times, hours of pain and, sorrow God wants us to put out trust in him and, come to him with our pains and, burdens in our prayers. In every situation that I have faced and, I still face, I got my greatest comfort, love and, support when I went before the throne of our Lord, in my prayers. I told God, all about the things that were binding me up inside and, giving me so much discomfort. You have read about the majority of the greatest challenges that I have faced in my life and, through it all, I never! Stopped praying, believing, trusting in God's words and, promises to see me through!.

Did I get weary? Yes I did, I became mentally exhausted, emotional, sick many days in my health and, I thought I was going to lose!

My mind!. Yes I had some good days, great days, and, extremely hard, trying days and, the attacks on my life and, my children's life, were hitting us back to back!. There were days that I felt like I was barely breathing as I said before. I would look around the room at others sometimes, just to see if people could actually see me, was I even alive?.

How did I get through those days, when I felt like everyone! Was against me and, I couldn't see my way out?. What did I do in those seconds, minutes, days, weeks, months and, years of despair?. I held on to my faith! Because my faith and, love for God was all! That I had! To get through those trials!. It was my faith that God would never! Forsake me, as everyone in my life had done. From a nine year old lost and, afraid little girl, who used to look out my bedroom window and, I would pray to the heavens and, stars for help at night, when I was afraid. I knew when I had fear, that if I could look up to the sky and, tell the Lord all about my fears. I knew in my heart that God was real, he did exist and, that God would hear my cries!.

I had faith in God before I even had an understanding of who God was, I just believed within my spirit that he was a loving God, he would never turn his ears and, heart away from me. If I did not believe that there was a God and, I lost my faith in him through my hurt and, pain, I probably would not be alive in my right mind today. I don't go to any rock! And, pray, no! I Go to the Lord! Our father, Jesus Christ in heaven, this is who I go to in my daily prayers for answers, guidance, direction and, for his unconditional love!.

You can go before the Lord, with all of your burdens, problems, pains, discouragement and, weariness too. God is waiting to hear you cry out to him, seek him in prayer and, for us to have belief and, have faith in him. It says, in Mathew Ch. 11 Vs. 28 Th 30 it reads, [28] Come unto me, all ye that labour and are heavy laden, and I will give you rest. [29] Take my yoke upon you, and learn of me; for I am meek and lowly in heart: and ye shall find rest unto your souls. [30] For my yoke is easy, and my burden is light. Amen!

Don't let the enemy or people discourage you against the will and, promises that the Lord has said for our lives. People will fail you, turn their backs on you and, lie to you at the blink of an eye. One day they may like you or love you and, the next minute that you do something that they don't like, people will turn that same care for you off, instantly!. That's not God's unconditional love at all.

You can't love someone today and, then when I don't perform the way that you want me to, now suddenly you don't like or love me anymore?. That is not a person that cares for your feelings or your heart and, that is not a form of God's love for one another, no!.

Unconditional love means that I am more concerned about the welfare of my partner, than I am for myself. It means that if loving you is not enough in our marriage, then I need to go before the throne of God and, ask God what more is it that I need to do, to get it!. That's how much you should love your spouse, you will go before the Lord and, ask God how and, what can I do, to love my spouse even more!.

Loving someone is selfless, meaning it's not all about you, but within a marriage it's about the US! Not I, but the US!. We both are loving each other, like a child's See/Saw on the playground. I'm going up! You go up! I'm going up! And, you're going! Up! Not one person in the marriage is leaving the other person behind!. We both are functioning in that relationship as a whole, in God's eyes we are "EQUAL"! Together!. Amen!..

If my husband is not feeling good and, my friends or family want me to come out, because it's the weekend, the answer is NO!. Why? Because that is my better half laying in the bed sick. That's my motivation! To be the best that I can be, that's my ride! Or die! Partner, when the world is fighting against me! And, the job is stressing me out.

That's my partner, my soft spot, my comfort when I come home from a horrible day, my spouse is my peace! When I make it back home! And, my children, as well, that's my family. So, if your spouse needs you, at their side when they are sick, mentally or emotionally going through something, the world should be dead! To you!. You need to be home, loving on my spouse!. This is the way a husband

and, wife should be towards each other in love today, having that selfless love! And, concerns, towards the wellbeing of each other's needs.

This is that part of having that unconditional love of God within. It's not about gifts, money or buying jewelry, cars and, clothes, we have replaced that unconditional love for eachother and, communication, with materialistic things and, looks!. The pleasures of the flesh! And, this selfish, evil spirit is destroying! Many families, relationships and, marriages today.

We are lacking God's unconditional love and, communication within our relationships with one another. Even with some Pastors, Bishops, Apostles and, Ministers in the ministry, many of them, in their marriages and, within their families are not! Showing their spouse and, their children, that unconditional love and, communication that is needed between everyone in the home.

We have to do a better job at communicating our feelings and, emotions to our spouse and, loved ones. The same way that we talk to our friends or coworkers about our problems, we should be communicating those same problems to our spouse and, loved ones that we love. We cannot read each other's minds and, cutting your voice off from speaking to your spouse, only allows the enemy to sneak into your relationship and, cause tension and, discouragement to the other spouse or person. You are treating your partner like an enemy, as if you careless about their feelings.

This is how marital affairs happen and, divorces happen, someone in that relationship felt as if they were not being heard and, they were not receiving the respect or love from their partner. So, in the midst of that hurt, anger and, pain, they sought comfort in someone else's arms. You do not want to shut your communication or voice down from your partner, you are hurting them by pushing them away from you. I did this many times within my two marriages, when my spouse would do something that offended me, I would mentally and, vocally shut down on them, because I felt like I had no voice, so, I stopped talking at times.

Did this help our marriage? No it did not, it just pushed the both of us further and, further away from each other.

In those times of distress and, problems in your marriage, families or with your children, we need to sit down with one another, turn the television and, radio off! Put the cell phones away!. Ask one another, how did we get here? And, where did the distress from our situations begin?. Then you both, take your time to discuss your thoughts about it and, begin to dissect those problems with one another. Start as a couple working together, on those thoughts, as to how you both can work out those issues together and, come to some common ground if you can. I tried my best, to savage both marriages, when I was married and, I even had the Bishop to counsel us, in both marriages, but, neither one of my husband's, wanted to come out from their sins. I was fighting for the marriage alone! And, you can't win, fighting alone!.

It may take a lot of quality time talking and, sharing your feelings with one another, as we know nothing happens overnight. But, if you both desire to stay together, do the work together and, are willing to put yourself aside and, now make it about US! And, not I!. Bring God into those discussions as well, this is first and, most important thing to do, don't leave God out of the discussion, like most people do. And, ask each other, would God want us tearing! One another down this way?. Read some scriptures, pertaining to what you may be facing within your problems, God's word has a way of healing our broken hearts, so, do not leave God out of resolving your problems.

Who do you think is responsible for this division within families, relationships and, marriages today?. Go back and read it again in Ephesians Ch. 6 Vs. 12 it reads, [12] For we wrestle not against flesh and blood, but against principalities, against powers, against the rulers of the darkness of this world, against spiritual wickedness in high places. Amen!

As I said before this spirit is bigger than us! And, in order for us to resist the Devil and, his attacks against ourselves and, our loved ones it says in the same Chapter of, Ephesians 6 Vs. 13 it reads, [13]

Wherefore take unto you the whole armor of God, that ye may be able to withstand in the evil day, and having done all, to stand. Amen!

Let us put on the whole armor of God daily in our lives, we fight the enemy with the Holy word of God! With the Spirit of God within us!. We trust God's mighty power! To cast the enemy back! To the Pits of hell! From whence he came from!. Pray for yourself in your prayers, your spouse, your children, your grandchildren, siblings, parents, family members and, your friends. And, talk to God alone, in a private area, where no distractions are around you. Talk to God, just like when you are sitting with a friend or family member talking to them and, you tell God everything that is on your heart. Give him all of your pain and, discomforts, because God loves you (Us) and, he wants to hear our voice, pleading our situations directly unto him. Amen!

God is our father, our daddy and, our everything!. And, you (We) can trust God with your situations and, wait for God to show you the next steps of your life, as he creates a new path for you. We have the right to petition God for anything that we want, that is in his holy will for us. It says in the scriptures in Philippians Ch 4 Vs. 6-7 it's reads, **6** Be careful for nothing; but in every thing by prayer and supplication with thanksgiving let your requests be made known unto God.**7** And the peace of God, which passeth all understanding, shall keep your hearts and minds through Christ Jesus. Amen!.

We need more strong men who have surrendered their life to Christ, helping to lead our homes and, families in Christ today. It says in the scriptures in 1 Corinthians Ch. 11 Vs. 2-3 it reads, **2** I praise you for remembering me in everything and for holding to the traditions just as I passed them on to you. **3** But I want you to realize that the head of every man is Christ, and the head of the woman is man,[a] and the head of Christ is God. Amen!

Until man returns back to his first love, which is Christ, being head of his life And, man being willing to walk upright in the commandments, principles and, values of the Holy word of God, the enemy will continue to try to kill! Steal! And, destroy! Our families, children, careers, health and, marriages, even more!.

A lot of our men, as well as women are broken, suffering from childhood trauma, drug addiction, alcoholism, pharmaceutical and, street pills. And, many other perverse addictions of sex, mental health issues and, violence. The devil knows our weaknesses and, he continues to lead our women, men and, children into this dark, evil, destructive system of this world. We as a people have to get our lives back covered and, surrender to God, to break these vitous! And, dangerous patterns, cycles and, behaviors within our lives and our families.

Our faith, hope and, trust should be always in the Lord, over everything in our lives and, within our marriages and, family. We cannot do anything without the help of the Lord. It says, in the scriptures in Isaiah Ch.12 Vs. 2 it reads, ² Behold, God is my salvation; I will trust, and not be afraid: for the LORD JEHOVAH is my strength and my song; he also is become my salvation. Amen!

Don't allow the enemy to discourage you and, keep you in fear, we have a mighty God that will fight our battles!. Even in your weakest moments, call on the name of the Lord, pick yourself up and, you start all over again!

You may have to go back to school as I did in my late thirties and, forties and, now my fifties, to advance yourself in your careers for you and, your family. I went back to school full time during the day and, I worked the night shift for many years, just so that I could get my college degrees and, change my field of work. Thank God, I found a university that only required me to attend classes, one day a week and, our other assignments were online.

You may have to search online for colleges, just like the university that I went to, that will benefit you being able to go to school and, work at the same time. Will it be hard, going back to school and, working? Yes it will! You will have to buckle down and, miss a lot of parties with family and, friends. You will have to focus on your studies, get the proper rest as well that you need and, even eat healthier to keep your energy level up!. Can it be done? Yes it can, I had three children, no family support and, no financial support from anyone. But, through my determination to change my story and, to aim higher for myself and, my family, I had to make some sacrifices to achieve my goals. The only person that can change your negative to a positive is you! (Us).

There were days that I wanted to give up on life, I felt like I just couldn't make it, but through discipline, commitment and, determination I did! It! And, I'm still doing it! Today! In 2025 and, beyond!. I claim it! believe! And, receive it! Amen!.

I am at a new beginning of my life, at fifty, one years young, starting a new thing, with God leading my steps. And, you can best believe that, I will not be slowing down, working towards my gift of being a successful author! From my childhood. My focus is to continue to work on my mental and, physical health, so that I can be physically and, mentally healthy for my next journeys, by also, eating healthy and, hitting that gym!. This is one of my many books that I will be writing and, publishing moving forward. This is book number two, I have two, more books coming out, by 2026 book three and four will be published as I said, Gods will. Please get all of my books, they will be a blessing for your lives, trust me they will be. I will continue as a Minister of God's army, serving his children in need and, spreading the good news! The gospel of Jesus Christ, everywhere that I go. This is my first! Mission, being commissioned! By God! To serve the Kingdom of the Lord!. Amen! There are lives to reach, teach, support and, as a fisherman of the Lord, I will seek all those that are willing to surrender their life to Christ, at their own will, to do so. God's work must always be first in our lives and, the mission continues to move forward!. As you can see, I have work to do and, as long as I keep Christ as head of my life and, environment, God will cover me and, see me through!.

It says, in the scriptures in Psalms Ch. 153 Vs. 7-8 it reads,

[7] Hear me speedily, O LORD: my spirit faileth: hide not thy face just from me, lest I be like unto them that go down into the pit. [8] Cause me to hear thy lovingkindness in the morning; for in thee do I trust: cause me to know the way wherein I should walk; for I lift up my soul unto thee. Amen! Call out the name of the Lord! In your time of need and,

God will answer us, within our spirit and, God will ask us, Where Art Thou!?. Amen!

As I said, the next few seconds of our lives are not promised to any of us. I pray that you, my readers, have taken notes, from many of the messages in this book and, you will apply some of these lessons and, messages to your lives, to not make some of the bad decisions and, choices that I made, without consulting God fist!. Amen!

I will leave some questions in the back of this book that can be a help and, guide towards you making the first steps, to begin the process of change for a better and, more fulfilled life. These are questions that you will ask yourself and, use the blank pages to write out how you will proceed. Better, yet get you a spiral, paper folder or a journal and, write out the questions from my book, if you don't want to write in this book and, begin answering those questions for yourself.

I can't map out your life for you, only you and, God knows what is best for you and, your journeys ahead. These questions as you answer them, will help you to identify some things about your life, who you are right now?. What areas of your life has hindered you and, what are your plans, towards reinventing yourself right now, towards change and, a better life for yourself?. I pray that this book of my journeys and, my life in Christ, will encourage you to not allow your past, to control you and, stop you from being who God has designed and, called you to be!. The only person that can make those changes and, you moving forward with your life, is you!. Trust in the word of God for your lives and, watch God see you through! As he did me!. Amen! I will leave you with this scripture:

Isaiah Ch. 41 Vs. 10 it reads,
[10] Fear thou not; for I am with thee: be not dismayed; for I am thy God: I will strengthen thee; yea, I will help thee; yea, I will uphold thee with the right hand of my righteousness. Amen!

Self reflection-Questions:

1. Think back in your life and, write out where you believe your first experience of trauma, pain or hurt began? .
2. How did that trauma make you feel! And, how did it affect you?.
3. How long have you allowed your traumatic experiences to affect you in your life, from moving forward?
4. How has that trauma stopped you from progressing past it and, growing?.
5. Who do you believe had a role to play in your trauma? And, what part of the trauma do you take accountability for, if any belongs to you?.
6. Now that you have identified when and, where your traumatic experiences came from, who played a role in your trauma? (Name the people or family members) and, what steps do you need to take, to forgive them?.
7. What are some of the things that you need to do, to get the help that you need for your trauma? Whether it be receiving counseling or psychological therapy, what steps do you need to take, to get the help for your healing?.
8. Are you willing to get the help that you need, to move forward in your life? And, why or why not?.
9. What goals and, visions do you have for your life, that you have not completed as of yet? And, are you willing to do the work, to accomplish your plans, or goals?.
10. Do you want to move forward to accomplish your goals, visions and, plans that you have for yourself and, how will you proceed?.
11. What steps are you willing to take and, sacrifices that you are willing to make, to move forward towards a healthier lifestyle?.
12. Who are the people, places and, things that are hindering you, mentally, emotionally and, physically? And, are you willing to

remove these toxic people, places or things from your life and, never look back!. (Just remember to call on the name of Jesus! To help you let them go and, God will give you the strength to move on!).
13. The last and, most important question that I ask is, have you surrendered your life over to Christ yet? Do you believe that Jesus Christ is the son of God? And, that Jesus Christ died for mankind's sins? And, that Jesus Christ rose on the third day?. Have you accepted Jesus Christ as your personal Lord and, Savior and, have you repented of your sins to God?. If you have done all of this, you have the Holy Spirit living with you and, your name is written! In the book of life! Amen!. This is all you have to say and, believe, to be welcomed into the Kingdom of God.

If you have not, I pray that you do it today, so that when you pass away, you will have an eternal place in heaven with Christ on the day of the Rapture!. Your name will forever! Be written in the book of life!. This is my prayer for you, your spouse, your children and, your grandchildren too. Establish yourself with a daily prayer life with our Lord and, savior Jesus Christ in heaven today and, watch your life begin to change, for your good!. Say this prayer with me, repeat after me here:

Ask God for forgiveness of your sins, repent to God, that you are a sinner, believe that Jesus Christ died on the cross for mankind's sins, believe that He is the son of God and, that Jesus Christ rose on the third day for you and, mankind's sins. If you said this prayer, you are now welcomed! Into the Kingdom of God!. I celebrate your victory! With you as my brother or sister in Christ. Welcome! My family! Into the Kingdom of God!. Amen!. This is it! And, walk Holy before the Lord!. Find you a good Bible teaching church as well, for you and, your family, to continue to be taught the word of God. Buy yourself a good Bible, a study Bible, a Bible concordance and, a Bible dictionary to help you study the word of God for yourself as well. Amen! There are Bible schools online and, many websites to help you dissect and, understand the word of God, that's what I did, for my own personal studies, as well. You can even pull up dictionaries and, study websites right from your cell phone, so, there is no excuse to not study to show yourself approved! As the Bible says. Amen! Please forgive yourself from all of your mistakes and, mishaps of life, because God still forgives and, love all! Of you!.

Thank you, my friends, for being my new readers and, friends in Christ. As I said, this is my second book published be looking out for both of my books coming your way on my website and other book outlets. I love you all! With the love of God! Many blessings to you and, your family.

"Miracle" My busy "Bee"

*My daughter Chanyka
and her father*

The Furnace heater I was burned on at 4

All the faces of myself then and now

*My father bought this bracelet for me
before he passed to Glory*

My only daughter "Princes Chanyka"

My three children and my "Mother Dear"

www.ingramcontent.com/pod-product-compliance
Lightning Source LLC
Chambersburg PA
CBHW071509150426
43191CB00009B/1463